THE COMPLETE IDIOT'S GUIDE® TO

Baby Brai Games

by Lawrence E. Shapiro, Ph.D., with Jennifer Lawler

ALPHA

A member of Penguin Group (USA) Inc.

To the memory of my mother, Frances Shapiro, who loved all the babies in the world, and most particularly, me. —LS

ALPHA BOOKS

Published by the Penguin Group

Penguin Group (USA) Inc., 375 Hudson Street, New York, New York 10014, USA

Penguin Group (Canada), 90 Eglinton Avenue East, Suite 700, Toronto, Ontario M4P 2Y3, Canada (a division of Pearson Penguin Canada Inc.)

Penguin Books Ltd., 80 Strand, London WC2R 0RL, England

Penguin Ireland, 25 St. Stephen's Green, Dublin 2, Ireland (a division of Penguin Books Ltd.)

Penguin Group (Australia), 250 Camberwell Road, Camberwell, Victoria 3124, Australia (a division of Pearson Australia Group Pty. Ltd.)

Penguin Books India Pvt. Ltd., 11 Community Centre, Panchsheel Park, New Delhi—110 017, India

Penguin Group (NZ), 67 Apollo Drive, Rosedale, North Shore, Auckland 1311, New Zealand (a division of Pearson New Zealand Ltd.)

Penguin Books (South Africa) (Pty.) Ltd., 24 Sturdee Avenue, Rosebank, Johannesburg 2196, South Africa

Penguin Books Ltd., Registered Offices: 80 Strand, London WC2R 0RL, England

Copyright © 2008 by Lawrence E. Shapiro, Ph.D.

International Standard Book Number: 978-1-59257-701-9
Library of Congress Catalog Card Number: 2007939620

10   09   08   8   7   6   5   4   3   2   1

Interpretation of the printing code: The rightmost number of the first series of numbers is the year of the book's printing; the rightmost number of the second series of numbers is the number of the book's printing. For example, a printing code of 08-1 shows that the first printing occurred in 2008.

Printed in the United States of America

Note: This publication contains the opinions and ideas of its authors. It is intended to provide helpful and informative material on the subject matter covered. It is sold with the understanding that the authors and publisher are not engaged in rendering professional services in the book. If the reader requires personal assistance or advice, a competent professional should be consulted.

The authors and publisher specifically disclaim any responsibility for any liability, loss, or risk, personal or otherwise, which is incurred as a consequence, directly or indirectly, of the use and application of any of the contents of this book.

Most Alpha books are available at special quantity discounts for bulk purchases for sales promotions, premiums, fund-raising, or educational use. Special books, or book excerpts, can also be created to fit specific needs.

For details, write: Special Markets, Alpha Books, 375 Hudson Street, New York, NY 10014.

Publisher: *Marie Butler-Knight*
Editorial Director: *Mike Sanders*
Senior Managing Editor: *Billy Fields*
Executive Editor: *Randy Ladenheim-Gil*
Development Editor: *Susan Zingraf*
Production Editor: *Kayla Dugger*

Copy Editor: *Catherine Schwenk*
Cartoonist: *Steve Barr*
Cover and Book Designer: *Becky Harmon*
Layout: *Becky Harmon, Ayanna Lacey*
Proofreaders: *Mary Hunt, Kayla Dugger*

Contents at a Glance

Contents

Appendixes

Introduction

Your new baby has an amazing year ahead of her, in which she'll learn everything from how to turn her head to how to cruise around the living room. Like most parents, you're probably anxious to help your baby develop her skills but unsure of the best ways to encourage and teach her. We're here to help.

Research shows that the more you talk to, sing to, and interact with your baby, the more successful he'll be in school and in his personal relationships. Who wouldn't want that for their baby? You probably already know how to relate to your baby—you can't help but smile when you see him wake up in the morning, and that teaches him that you love him. When he smiles back, you give him a hug and tell him what a sweetie he is. That's how he learns about social interactions, and you can bet you'll get an even brighter smile next time.

But sometimes, especially as new parents, we don't quite trust ourselves to know what to do or how best to stimulate our baby's senses, challenge her brain, and teach her what she needs to know to interact effectively with the world around her.

That's why this book can help. We'll show you what you need to know about how your baby's brain develops, including milestones you should be aware of. We'll show you games and activities you can do with your baby to help him explore and develop a full range of skills. We'll also help you adapt the games and activities for a baby with special needs.

How This Book Is Organized

The Complete Idiot's Guide to Baby Brain Games is divided into six parts, each covering a different area of skill development. You can read it from start to finish, or you can just turn directly to the information you need most.

Part 1, "Teaching Your Baby Through Games," introduces you to the developmental milestones a typical baby goes through, and shows you how to keep your play with your baby safe and fun. How does your baby's brain develop? What makes your infant go from a sleepy newborn to a climbing, crawling, cruising toddler? What kinds of games and activities can you use to help stimulate your baby's brain?

Part 2, "Teaching Your Baby Language," illustrates how to help your baby understand what you're saying to him. Your young baby may not seem to be paying attention, but he is listening to every word you say. At this age, his ability to understand will far outstrip his ability to communicate what he wants and needs, but we'll show you games and activities to use to help him learn to communicate with words. This part also offers ways to help your baby learn about himself.

Part 3, "Teaching Your Baby to Think," provides games and activities you can use to help improve your baby's ability to recall and remember things, reason out solutions to problems, and explore the world around her. For your baby to learn about the world, she needs to understand not what to think, but how to think.

Part 4, "Stimulating Your Baby's Social and Emotional Development," shows you games and activities you can use to help your baby calm down once he's gotten wound up, and get him started on learning how to self-calm—if baby isn't happy, nobody is happy. We'll also give you games and activities to help your baby develop independence and self-help skills, plus we'll show you how you can help your baby imitate and pretend—crucial skills for social interactions.

Part 5, "Stimulating Your Baby's Sensory Development," offers games and activities you can use to help your baby use her senses of smell, taste, sight, sound, and touch. We tend to think of encouraging our babies' motor skills and thinking skills, but it's equally important to encourage the exploration and development of the five senses.

Part 6, "Developing Your Baby's Physical Skills," has games and activities that will help your baby develop the body strength, balance, and other abilities he needs for his gross motor skills. Your newborn baby is a pretty helpless handful of needs—with these games, your baby can develop his motor skills, which in turn makes him more independent. We also provide games and activities that will help him begin to master fine motor skills, such as using his hands to reach for and grasp objects.

Extras

You'll also find additional information, warnings, anecdotes, and tips about playing with your child in little boxes throughout the book. Here's what they are:

 **BABY BABBLE**

Definitions for jargon and expressions related to your baby's development.

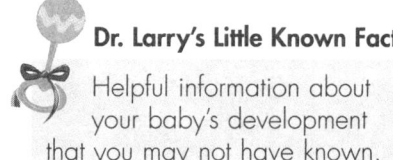 **Dr. Larry's Little Known Facts**

Helpful information about your baby's development that you may not have known.

Brainy Baby

Tidbits, wisdom, and tips that help you understand your baby's brain development, plus ways to use the games most effectively.

Baby Beware

Special warnings and cautions about what not to do—because some ways of playing with your baby could be ineffective or could actually endanger your child.

Acknowledgments

We'd like to thank our agent, Marilyn Allen, for all her hard work. Our editor at Alpha, Randy Landenheim-Gil, has been an enormous help from the beginning. Dr. Larry would also like to acknowledge the thousands of parents he has met, who have made raising happy and healthy children their number-one priority.

Trademarks

All terms mentioned in this book that are known to be or are suspected of being trademarks or service marks have been appropriately capitalized. Alpha Books and Penguin Group (USA) Inc. cannot attest to the accuracy of this information. Use of a term in this book should not be regarded as affecting the validity of any trademark or service mark.

Part 1

Teaching Your Baby Through Games

What's going on in there? You look down at your newborn, and you have to wonder what's happening that makes her blink and take notice of the world around her.

This part of the book shows you how your baby's brain develops, how every experience contributes to the wiring that your baby's brain is building, and gives you an idea of how to use the games and activities in this book to stimulate your baby's brain.

How Your Baby's Brain Develops

In This Chapter

- ◆ Recognizing how connections and pathways are formed in your baby's brain
- ◆ Identifying types of stimulation that help your baby's brain work more efficiently
- ◆ Understanding milestones in your baby's development
- ◆ Finding out about developmental concerns
- ◆ Adapting games and activities for a special needs baby

You've probably heard this one a few times: "Babies don't come with an instruction manual!" If you're feeling that way, you've come to the right place. This book will help you learn ways to interact with your baby that will help your baby grow mentally, physically, emotionally, and socially.

Because babies come in both boy and girl models, we interchange "he" and "she" throughout the book to refer to them.

In this chapter, we show you how your baby's brain is formed through the experiences that she has during the first few years of her life. We explain the importance of stimulating your baby's brain in "good" ways, through challenging games and activities that she'll enjoy even as she learns.

We also describe the developmental stages a baby typically goes through, and offer information on what to do if you suspect a developmental delay. Finally, we discuss how you can adapt the games and activities in this book to suit a baby with special needs.

Forging Pathways and Connections

Not so long ago, most researchers believed that the brain your baby had at birth was the one he was stuck with for life. But new studies show that from birth until about age three, your baby's brain undergoes dramatic changes as it creates pathways and connections to form tiny, intricate networks—the "wiring" that shapes how your baby will think, speak, reason, feel, and behave.

Babies who aren't stimulated and challenged as these connections are being made are less likely to develop to their full potential, learn the skills they need to do well in school, get along well with others, and lead rewarding and satisfying lives.

Linking—and Losing—Brain Cells

At birth, your baby has more than 100 billion brain cells. (For purposes of comparison, it took Crayola 93 years to make 100 billion crayons). So from the start, the most important pathways and connections are already in place—the connections that regulate the basics of your baby's physical functioning (heartbeat, breathing, and reflexes, among others).

As your baby explores the world and learns about it—and about herself and her relationship to the world—a process of weeding out takes place in her brain. Her brain eliminates the connections that she doesn't use very often to make room for the connections that she does use, or at least uses more frequently.

Every experience that your baby has, good or bad, affects the connections that his brain builds. All babies create unique brains through the connections they make from their experiences. Because your baby experiences the world through his five senses, it's important to stimulate him through all of them—taste, smell, sound, sight, and touch. Because experiences come from the senses, a baby with a visual impairment, for example, won't build the same kinds of connections in his brain that a baby who can see perfectly will.

If you stimulate useful connections in the following ways, your baby's brain learns how to think and organize experiences effectively:

- Playing physical games helps create connections that build motor skills.

- Talking and reading to babies help them develop connections that build language skills.

- Showing loving affection to babies helps develop connections that build emotional responses.

- Doing all of the above will—you guessed it—give babies all of the above skills.

Recognizing Good Stimulation

Good stimulation comes from experiences that challenge your baby's brain. These experiences build connections that make your baby's brain faster and more efficient. That doesn't mean that you need to enroll your baby in an academic program before she's two months old. It just means that she should be exploring, experiencing, and interacting with her world—and the people in it. Keep her safe, by all means, but let her get her hands on the things around her.

The games and activities throughout the book, starting in Chapter 4, all promote good stimulation. You don't have to play the games exactly as described—pay attention to your baby and modify the games as needed to make them interesting and appropriate for your child.

Limiting Not-So-Good Stimulation

There are stimulations around you and your baby that don't challenge the brain. For example, sitting in front of the television doesn't stimulate your baby's brain the way that playing a memory game with you does, and may, in fact, do some harm.

Below the age of two, your baby shouldn't spend *any* time in front of a television screen, according to the American Academy of Pediatrics. Those baby DVDs and television shows may seem educational, but they're not good for your baby.

A recent study conducted by researchers at the University of Washington showed that babies who spent a lot of time in front of the television (including watching videos or DVDs) had slower language development. The study concluded that every hour that a young child watches television (or videos/DVDs) reduces his vocabulary by six to eight words. That's a great argument for unplugging the television and digging out some cards and books.

One Step at a Time: Developmental Milestones

During the amazing first year of life, your baby will go from helpless newborn to toddler-wannabe, scooting around the house. She'll learn everything from how to hold her head up, to how to eat with a spoon, to how to pull up to a standing position. And that's not all! She'll learn how to understand many words and even how to say a few. She'll also start learning about social interactions. The first year is a very active time in your baby's brain development, to say the least.

The following is a rough guideline of when a baby typically learns various skills.

Developmental Milestones

The following timetable shows some of the major developmental skills—including motor, auditory and language, visual, thinking and self-awareness, and emotional—for a "typical" baby. Your baby may not mature at this exact pace, but this list provides you with a handy guide for knowing what developments you can expect from her at a certain age.

At 1 month:

- Lift her head for short periods when on her tummy
- Respond to your voice
- Suck and swallow appropriately
- Stare at faces

At 2 months:

- Realize he has hands
- Track objects
- Make sounds besides crying
- Smile at you when you smile at him

At 3 months:

- Kick her legs
- Reach for objects held in front of her
- Grasp an object handed to her
- Recognize your face
- Turn toward a sound

At 4 months:

- Roll over (tummy to back)
- Lift head to 90 degrees
- Respond to shapes and colors
- Communicate his needs by crying
- Explore objects by putting them in her mouth
- Use crying to communicate her needs

At 5 months:

- Attend to small objects
- See across the room

- Notice differences in bright colors
- Explore cause and effect (i.e., dropping food from his high chair)

At 6 months:

- Sit by herself either independently or with little support for a few moments
- Make sounds of more than one syllable
- Use consonant sounds
- Hold a bottle, if bottle-fed
- Copy a few facial expressions

At 7 months:

- Self-feed finger foods
- Try to get object that is out of his reach
- Show interest in looking in a mirror
- Understand emotion by your tone of voice
- Imitate many sounds

At 8 months:

- Start crawling
- Respond differently to different people
- Sit unsupported
- Respond to his own name
- Say "ma-ma" and "da-da" interchangeably

At 9 months:

- Shift from lying on tummy to sitting by himself
- Use pincer grasp to pick up very small objects
- Drop objects and then look for them
- Use many different sounds and syllables in babbling

At 10 months:

- Stand holding onto something
- Pull herself to standing position
- Realize that items don't stop existing just because he can't see them (object permanence)
- Express being upset if a toy is taken away

At 11 months:

- Wave good-bye
- Say "ma-ma" and "da-da" appropriately
- Roll or throw a ball

At 12 months:

- From a standing position, move from one piece of furniture to another—"cruising"
- Understand the function of familiar objects
- Imitate activities
- Want mother or primary caregiver over others
- Show interest in "reading" books with you
- Show attachment to specific objects

What If I Think My Baby Has a Problem?

Because all babies develop at different rates, it's best to only use the developmental milestones such as those provided here as a rough guide. Though typically developing babies all go through the same stages, they go through them at different rates, and there's a broad range of "typical." Babies also progress differently depending on their personalities and interests.

However, because parents are the ones most likely to notice a developmental delay in their baby, it's important for you to recognize when a delay seems to be occurring, and to seek further evaluation for your baby. Remember that most babies develop just fine, and for those who do have delays, many catch up with no significant problems.

Keeping a journal is helpful if you have concerns about your baby. In the journal, you can ...

- Note what questions you have and why you're concerned.

- Record what your baby is doing (or isn't doing), track development, and/or make a keepsake.

- Note behaviors over the course of several days or weeks before you visit with your baby's pediatrician to help you clarify and express your concerns.

- Keep track of what's happening with your baby if your pediatrician suggests giving him a little more time before recommending a full developmental evaluation.

Types of Developmental Problems

If your baby does have a *developmental delay*, seek treatment and advice right away, when it makes the most difference to your baby's immediate health as well as her future well-being.

Delays can occur in several different areas of a baby's physical, mental, and emotional development. A baby can have one or more areas of delay, including:

- Gross motor skills, such as crawling or walking

- Fine motor skills, such as grasping a toy

- Understanding language

- Communicating or expressing language

- Self-help skills, such as feeding herself

- Social skills, such as playing with others

- Emotional skills, such as identifying his own emotions and responding to emotions in others

A global developmental delay (sometimes called pervasive developmental disorders or PDDs) means your baby has delays in all of these areas of development. Often such global delays are caused by a physical disorder, such as a brain abnormality or a chromosomal disorder. They can also be caused by prematurity. A full evaluation by specialists can help determine if there's a physical cause of the developmental delay.

About 1 to 3 percent of children have global developmental delays, whereas about 15 percent of school-aged children have developmental delays in just one or two areas. Many of these children "catch up" over time, while others can learn strategies to help them work around the problem.

If you think your baby may have a delay, the best thing to do is check with your pediatrician. A thorough evaluation will help you decide the best course of action.

Making Accommodations for Babies with Special Needs

Learning that your baby has special needs can come as a shock. Most parents need time—not to mention a little help—to learn how to cope with the differences their baby with special needs has. It's important for you to inform yourself about your baby's problems, how they can best be treated, and what you can do to help. Don't forget to access community resources and ask for the assistance that you need.

Under the Individuals with Disabilities Education Act (IDEA), your special needs baby is entitled to early intervention services from birth, through the Early Intervention Program (IEP). These services include:

- Education, counseling, and support groups (for the family)
- Special instruction
- Speech therapy
- Audiology services
- Occupational and physical therapy
- Psychological, nursing, and social work services
- Vision services
- Assistive devices

Your pediatrician or local school district office should be able to refer you to the appropriate place for more information.

Typically, developing babies want to explore the world. Special needs babies may not have that innate drive and therefore must be encouraged to reach out and experience the world around them.

Babies with special needs often require more time and repetition to learn a new skill. It's important to allow your baby the space and time she needs to acquire the skill, without showing your frustration or disappointment if she's not moving as fast as other babies are.

As parents, we tend to do more for our special needs babies than we probably should because of the challenges we know they face. Consult with your medical team to learn the best ways you can encourage and support your baby with special needs as he learns and grows. Staying positive helps your baby and those around him do their best.

Your special needs baby still requires—and deserves—as much love and attention as any other child. Many of the games that we describe in this book can be adapted to suit babies with different types of challenges.

Premature Babies

Premature babies generally progress along the same lines as full-term babies, unless they are very premature or have other medical issues surrounding their premature birth.

For premature babies with no other challenges, you may only need to adapt the games by adjusting the age range in which you introduce them. If your three-month-old was born six weeks premature, she may not be ready for games for three-month-olds until an additional six weeks have passed. For example, you might not expect her to babble to get attention until closer to eight months rather than at six months.

> **Brainy Baby**
>
> Games and activities that encourage bonding, trust, and reassurance (see Chapter 13) can help premature babies cope with the demands of being born early.

If your premature baby has additional challenges, read on for ways to adapt the games and activities to suit your baby's other challenges.

Physically Challenged Babies

Babies may have physical challenges ranging from a cleft palate, which makes sucking and swallowing difficult; to cerebral palsy, which makes motor control difficult. Depending on your baby's situation, you may be able to play some—or even many—of the games without modification.

For example, a baby with a visual impairment will still delight in hearing you say his name (see Chapter 4, "Conversations with Your Baby") and listening to what you say about him (see Chapter 4, "Baby's Eavesdropping Game"). By the same token, a child with low vision still needs to make the most of the vision he has, so you'll still want to play games that stimulate his vision (see Chapter 15).

For a baby who has difficulty with motor skills, the "Nature Walk Game" in Chapter 15, which stimulates vision, can be done from a stroller or a wheelchair, or while being carried.

Discuss your baby's physical limitations with her pediatrician. It may be a good idea to ask for a referral to a physical or occupational therapist who will help you learn how to interact physically with your baby in effective ways. As you grow accustomed to your baby and become more familiar with her ways and her needs, you will become more confident in how you play with her.

You can also bring this book with you and show some of the games to your baby's pediatrician or physical/occupational therapist and ask how they suggest you adapt the games for your baby.

Babies with Cognitive Challenges

Babies with cognitive impairments need play, love, and interaction with their parents even more than the typical baby. For most games, you'll probably need to discard the age range suggested, as your baby won't be quite ready for some of the challenges.

While you don't want to understimulate your baby, overwhelming him with challenges he can't possibly meet doesn't help him in the long run. Instead, consider what your baby can do, and find games that seem suitable for his abilities. Most of the games with the age range "from birth and up" should be fine for your baby, so start with those and work your way through the others.

Babies with cognitive impairments can and do master new skills all the time, but it may take longer for them than for other babies, and they may need significantly more repetition than another baby might. Keep this in mind as you play.

Introduce games and see what your baby thinks. Give her a few tries before going on to something else. Simplify the games so that she doesn't have to follow too many directions in a row or try to accomplish too many tasks at once. For example:

- In "Puzzle Game" (see Chapter 19), use one puzzle with only four or five pieces. Go on to more complex puzzles only after your baby masters the simple puzzle.

- In "March to the Music Game" (see Chapter 20), you might start with identifying when the music is on and when it's off before adding the physical component of marching to the music.

A child development specialist may be a good resource for you to consult. They often have suggestions for ways to interact with your baby to help his brain grow and develop.

Babies with Multiple Needs

Some children have more than one challenge to face. Babies with global developmental delay may have difficulties with physical skills as well as mental and emotional skills. In that case, you'll want to ignore the age range suggested for the games and focus on finding games appropriate for your baby's abilities.

Many of the simple sensory games are fine for babies with multiple challenges. For example, massaging your baby as described in "Small Circle Massage," "Gentle Squeeze Massage," and "Fingertip Brush Massage" (see Chapter 17) are nice ways to give your baby a loving touch. Any child may enjoy "The Itsy Bitsy Spider Game" (see Chapter 17).

Other games can be modified, depending on your baby's needs. Speak with your baby's pediatrician and physical/occupational therapist for ways to adapt the games to suit your baby.

The Least You Need to Know

- Every experience your baby has shapes her brain and contributes to the network of connections she makes.

- Some types of stimulation are better for your baby's brain than others.

- Babies typically develop in identifiable stages, though rates of progress can vary. Your baby can be more advanced in one area and less in another depending on his interests.

- Most parents have some concern about their baby's development, but most babies progress just fine on their own time table.

- Babies with special needs can benefit from playing games and activities just as typically developing babies do; the games can be adapted to suit their needs.

There Are Many Ways to Be Smart

In This Chapter

- ◆ Understanding what "intelligence" means and how you can help your baby develop it

- ◆ Recognizing different kinds of intelligence and fostering your baby's gifts

- ◆ Understanding the importance of creativity in your baby's life

- ◆ Encouraging your baby's social life—even with separation anxiety

- ◆ Exposing your baby to a wide variety of experiences to bolster her brain power

The definition of intelligence is hazy—what qualities or skills make a baby intelligent? In this chapter, we describe what we mean by intelligence and let you know why we think that playing games with your baby will help him improve his thinking power.

We also explore the theory of multiple intelligences, and why there's more than one way to be smart. You'll even learn how you can help your baby develop his intelligence in whichever way it presents itself.

Helping your baby develop into an intelligent human being doesn't just require knowledge found on IQ tests. We also describe ways to bolster your baby's creativity—and why it's important to do so—and explain why your baby needs to hang out with lots of other people (even though we know you're awesome at providing for all of his needs).

Can I Improve My Baby's Intelligence?

The title of this book suggests that by playing games and doing certain activities with your baby, you can help him become "smarter." In other words, you can help him increase his intelligence. But what exactly does that mean? And will the games really help you do that?

What Is Intelligence?

When people use the word "intelligence" (and related words like "smart" and "clever"), they usually mean some sort of general ability to reason, make decisions, solve problems, conceive of abstractions, learn new information (and put it to use), adapt to circumstances, and apply past experiences to present situations—with bonus points for avoiding painful experiences in the first place through the use of any of the aforementioned skills.

When professionals refer to a child's IQ (intelligence quotient), they are referring to numbers derived from standardized intelligence tests, which are sometimes used with infants but are more commonly employed with school-aged children.

Ordinary people—that is, not researchers investigating how the brain works—tend to focus on things like common sense, verbal ability, computational ability, competence in the tasks of daily life (including social interactions), and thirst for knowledge. That's good enough for us!

Does Playing Games Increase Intelligence?

The truth is, most typically developing babies have an innate drive to master the language, motor, and cognitive skills they need to become independent little critters. So why do we think you should play games with your baby?

Because, as we discussed in Chapter 1, research shows that babies build their brains based on what they learn through the experiences that they have. If you play physical games with your baby, for example, she develops motor skill connections. Research also shows that babies whose parents talk to, sing to, read to, and interact with them in general do better overall in terms of health and success than babies whose parents don't do these things.

Why Play Games with Your Baby?

Now it's true that you don't have to actually play games with your baby in order to interact with him, but we still think it's a great idea to do so, for these reasons:

- ♦ Games are a simple means of organizing your efforts in an effective way.

- ♦ Playing games is always enjoyable—for babies and their parents—and allows opportunities for shared experiences, bonding, and trust building.

- ♦ With many of the games, you can invite other children to join in, making them a good way to share family time and build bonds between siblings.

- ♦ Once you've learned how to play the games, you can incorporate them into your daily life. You don't have to make a play date with your daughter to get in a few minutes of peek-a-boo.

- ♦ Game playing may remind you to encourage your baby to develop some skills that you may otherwise not think about. For example, a quiet reader may not think about playing boisterous "chase me" games with his baby, but babies love such games!

Brainy Baby

Research has shown that the more time you spend playing with your baby or in one-on-one interactions with her, the more you stimulate her brain and help it forge valuable connections she'll need to do well in life.

◆ Finally, thinking in terms of games and activities reminds you to spend time doing these things (talking, singing, reading, and so on) with your baby.

Exposing Your Baby to Many Experiences

How can you nurture the various kinds of intelligence your baby may have? By using and exposing your baby to music, art, role playing, hands-on experiences, and field trips to help her exercise all of her senses and experience the world around her. Through exposure to a variety of experiences, she can express her unique intelligence.

Your baby's brain builds connections based on the experiences that she has. New and interesting people, places, and things help her build valuable connections.

What are some of the experiences a young baby can appreciate and learn from? Even something as simple as pushing your baby in his stroller as you go for a walk lets him experience the outside world—seeing the trees, hearing the birds, feeling the wind on his face, smelling the neighbor's charcoal grill, trying to eat the leaf that you just showed him. Go with a friend and let your baby also listen to you talk to each other, to him, and about him. For your baby, that's a lot of action to pack into a simple stroll around the block.

You don't have to spend a lot of money flying your baby to Paris to give her experiences worth having:

◆ Turn chores into an opportunity to give your baby a new experience. Going to the grocery store may be a tedious errand you have to run, but to your baby, it's an exciting place full of delightful sights, smells, and sounds. Talk to your baby about what you're doing as you fill your cart.

◆ Go on field trips with your baby. Take him to the zoo, to the mall, or to grandma's house.

◆ Look for baby-friendly activities in your community, such as story time at the public library, or Mommy-and-me dance or exercise sessions at the local studio or gym.

Baby Beware

Don't forget that your baby is just a baby and doesn't have the stamina of an adult. Too many experiences crammed together can overstimulate your baby and make him unhappy and fussy. Give him time to process a new experience before setting out on another adventure.

Appreciating the Importance of Creativity

Creativity isn't just about painting pictures. It's about finding new ways of doing things and applying new ways of thinking to old problems. Creativity is fundamental to growth and learning. To be creative requires imagination; it also requires a willingness to be out of the ordinary.

That's why creativity can actually, sometimes, be hard for parents to encourage in their children, because schools and workplaces often value conformity over creativity. We may think it's better for our children to be regarded as successful in school and work than to be creative there—and sometimes the two are, or at least seem to be, mutually exclusive (depending on the school and the work, of course).

Creativity allows your child to solve problems, adapt to new situations, and change the way she thinks based on information she encounters.

It Takes a Village: Encouraging Interactions with Others

Babies are social creatures from birth. Studies show that babies would rather look at people than objects, so socializing seems to be innate—babies want to be with other people. At first, these other people are mostly parents or caregivers, but over time, babies become interested in the larger world and the people in it, and start to enjoy spending time with them. Such social interactions help your baby's emotional and cognitive growth.

One way that new parents often introduce their babies to other people is by joining or creating play groups or going on play dates. Though this can be a good way for you to meet like-minded parents, don't expect your baby to interact with other babies. If you put two babies in a room with toys, they won't play together. They may not even look at each other. Child-to-child socialization happens later on. But babies love to play with older children and adults.

Though you may be her primary caregiver, it's important for your baby to experience all kinds of relationships with many different people. Otherwise, what she learns about the world is limited to what she can learn from you. She needs to experience a wide variety of people and responses to learn how to deal with the world on her own, as she'll have to as she grows older.

Different people have different ways of relating to your baby, and most of those ways teach him something useful. Mom may be the one your baby turns to when he's upset or hungry, but Dad is the one who flies him around the room like he's a supersonic jet—and having both experiences is important for his growth and development.

Your baby learns how to socialize with other people by watching and interacting with you. When she's a few months old, she'll become interested in other people, including strangers waiting in line at the bank. She'll also learn to imitate what you do, such as waving bye-bye to people.

But when he reaches about seven months, *separation anxiety* often sets in. He may cry if anyone but his parents holds him. This makes it difficult for him to socialize with other people—and may hurt other people's feelings (especially grandparents and other close family members).

BABY BABBLE

Separation anxiety is your baby's unwillingness to let you out of her sight. It occurs because she's starting to realize that she is a separate person from you. At the same time, she knows you're her primary source of all good things. If you leave, she doesn't know when or if you'll return—so it's in her best interest to try to prevent your leaving. Some babies don't have much anxiety, while others have a great deal. And some older babies (toddler age and preschool) may have separation anxiety, especially during periods of stress, such as having a new caregiver, having a new sibling at home, moving, or other life stressors.

What can you do to encourage your baby to socialize even when he's feeling anxious? Try the following:

- Explain to other people that your baby is having separation anxiety so they don't try to force unwanted attention on her.

- Encourage people to talk with him and play with him while he's in your arms or sitting in your lap (what he regards as the safest place).

- Give her time to warm up by letting her explore the environment without people picking her up or blocking her view of her parents.

If you're leaving your baby (such as at day care or Grandma's house), these are helpful strategies to ease the anxiety:

- Leave after your baby has eaten and when he feels rested.

- Have a good-bye ritual. Don't just disappear—this makes her feel even more anxious—but do say good-bye calmly and leave.

- Practice with being gone only short periods at first, so that he learns you're coming back.

By encouraging your baby to interact with others, you'll be helping her prepare for a lifetime of interacting with others successfully and doing it in a rewarding and fulfilling way.

The Least You Need to Know

- Your baby is smart in a number of different ways.

- Playing games and activities with your baby helps him build his intelligence.

- By exposing your baby to new experiences, you help her understand the world around her and forge important connections in her brain.

- Your baby needs to socialize with people other than you to see the "big picture."

- If you encourage your baby's creativity, you can help him become adept at solving problems and facing challenges.

3

Developing Your Baby's Brain Through Play

In This Chapter

- ◆ Using games to help you and other family members bond with your baby

- ◆ Learning to trust your instincts when it comes to your baby

- ◆ Understanding your baby's responses to play

- ◆ Keeping play safe and fun for everyone

- ◆ Realizing that playtime with your baby has its limits

It's important to recognize your baby's responses and respect what she likes and doesn't like. We give you tips on how to figure that out. We also show you how to be a good role model for your baby, because one of the most important ways she learns is through imitation.

In this chapter, we show you how to use games to help everyone in the family bond with your baby. We also encourage you to trust your instincts when it comes to playing with your baby. We also illustrate how to keep play safe and fun for everyone involved, and give you the lowdown on the limits of play.

Bonding with Your Baby

Playing games with your baby gives you the opportunity to bond with him. Other family members can also build bonds with the baby by joining in the play. In fact, game playing can be a wonderful way for dads and siblings to bond with the baby, especially if Mom is breastfeeding and they don't get the opportunity to feed the baby.

How Bonding Works

Bonding is an ongoing process that occurs naturally over time as your baby and her caregivers interact. It isn't something that happens in a few minutes right after birth, and it isn't something only mothers can or need to do. By taking care of your baby, responding to her needs, and showing her how much you love her through cuddles and words, you, and others, will establish a strong bond.

Bonding Through Play

In your baby's early months, bonding can be strengthened by playing games and doing activities that involve touching. Babies readily respond to skin-to-skin contact, so cuddling and massages are in order.

Games that encourage eye contact also help with bonding. Babies love faces, and they try to imitate what they see. Don't forget to talk or sing to your baby as you play your games. Look through this book for games appropriate for the age range of "from birth and up" for suggestions on things to do to help you (and others) bond with your young baby.

Brainy Baby

Bonding with your baby is easier if you feel like you have help and support. Enlist whatever assistance you need to take care of your baby and the other obligations you have (like keeping the house clean and the dog fed). If you don't feel like you're bonding with your baby, talk it over with your pediatrician. He has experience dealing with just these kinds of issues and can offer suggestions and resources.

Trusting Your Instincts

As you interact with your baby, you naturally talk to him in a way he finds pleasing (see Chapter 4), and cuddle with him in a way that makes him feel reassured. Most likely, no one had to instruct you in how to do that.

In fact, your instincts as a parent are pretty darn good, so trust them when it comes to playing with your baby. Games that you enjoy and that your baby seems to enjoy are preferable to games that you don't like or that bore your baby.

Let your parenting instincts count for something and learn to trust them. If you think a game is too advanced for your baby, though she's in the age range for it, then wait and introduce it later. If you think an activity we suggest is stupid, then hey, we're okay with the idea of you never trying it. Every baby is different (as is every parent) and you know your baby best. Engage your baby's senses and play with her in the ways that *you* think make the most sense.

Paying Attention to Your Baby's Responses

As you play with your baby, make sure you're paying attention to his responses. Overstimulating or overtiring your baby makes him fussy and irritable, which in turn may make you fussy and irritable.

Most of the games in this book are meant to be played for a few minutes (or even a few seconds!), not for half an hour. You can play them off and on throughout the day, but don't think that you have to schedule an hour-long play date with your baby every afternoon. Though your baby loves her one-on-one time with you, actual active play doesn't have to take up every minute of that time.

It's also tempting to try a lot of different activities and games with your baby to see which ones she likes and responds best to. But try not to introduce too many new things to her at once. Give her time to think about what she has experienced before introducing another game, activity, or stimulating experience. Try one game at a time, repeat it a few times, figure out if she likes it or not, then go do something else for a while (and remember to take your baby with you!).

As you play with your baby, ensure that you make eye contact with him (he loves that and learns from it), that you talk or sing to him (he loves that, too!), and that you watch for his responses—and respond back to them.

Recognizing Your Baby's Likes and Dislikes

Your baby needs to know that you will respect her likes and dislikes (when it comes to game-playing, not when it comes to whether she has to go to the doctor or not). This is one of the ways she develops trust in you and one of the ways that you can reassure her that you care about her.

However, sometimes your baby's responses can be a bit subtle, and you may not know how to interpret them yet. A smile and a giggle—yeah, anyone can figure out what that means! But other than that, because he can't talk to you yet, how do you know what he's thinking?

If your baby has lost interest in the game, the signs may be subtle. She may simply stop cooperating, despite your encouragement. Other signs that your baby is tired and it's probably time for you to stop an activity are:

- Fussing, whining, and crying
- Unfocused looks
- Looking away
- Turning away
- Back arching as she tries to get away

- Making unpleasant faces (instead of smiling or seeming interested)

- Clenching his fists

- Waving her arms and legs around

- Rubbing his eyes

- Pulling her ears, nose, or hair (or yours)

- Yawning (right, this one isn't exactly subtle, but we're including it anyway)

- Clinging more than usual

Brainy Baby

Typical signs that your baby is still interested in the game you're playing include: wide eyes, attending to you (or an object you're presenting to her), smiling at you, and reaching for an object.

Stop the game and give her a break, or try a different game if you think she would be interested in doing something else.

It's important to respond to your baby's cues because this is how he learns to communicate with you. If his cues don't seem to make any difference, he may stop trying to communicate.

Modeling Constructive Play

One of the most important ways your baby learns is through imitation. How else would she learn to talk? She learns many of her behaviors by watching you—and she's always watching you. (Okay, maybe not when she's asleep in the other room. But still, she watches you a lot.)

You're his primary teacher, so teach him well. Show him what you're doing, even if you think he's too young to understand. Describe why you do the things you do and make the decisions you make, even if he hasn't progressed further in his communication with you than cooing at you. Your baby understands far more than you think, and getting into the habit of being a good role model now only helps you down the road.

When it comes to playing games, your baby may need some instruction. That doesn't mean reading the directions to her (though you can). It means showing her what to do, guiding her as she tries, and giving her feedback ("Good job!" or "Try again!").

Repetition is an incredibly important part of the learning process. It can seem frustrating when you show your baby how to play a game one day and the next day he looks at you like he's never played the game before. But it takes a while for your baby to learn and remember, and it's up to you to teach him how. Getting frustrated or deciding not to bother doesn't help him. Being willing to try, try again does.

Keeping Play Safe and Fun

Playing with your baby should be an enjoyable experience for both of you (or all of you, if you're making it a family affair). It should also be *safe*. Some of the games suggest that you use materials that shouldn't be left with your baby unsupervised. Follow those safety instructions carefully.

If you don't understand how to play a game, then try a different game. If the way you think you're supposed to play one of the games seems potentially dangerous, don't play it. We have been careful to include only games that are tried-and-true, but all babies and parents are different, so choose your games and activities as you see fit.

Baby-Proofing Your Home

Because your baby learns by doing and exploring, throughout this book we encourage you to give your baby the freedom to do so. Because your baby doesn't know any better about putting things in her mouth (this is also how she learns), it's crucial for your house to be safe for your baby.

Baby-proofing your home graduates to toddler-proofing when your baby begins to walk. In other words, keeping your home safe for your baby is an ongoing process. It's not something you do once and never have to think about again. As your baby's skills develop, he is exposed to more potential dangers, and you have to install more safety devices or be more careful about where you leave potentially dangerous objects.

Using Safe Materials

Some of the games in this book require materials and toys. Make sure that you always use safe materials and objects for the games. This means that toys and objects should not be a choking hazard for your baby. (That is, they should not be able to fit into a toilet paper tube—if they do, they're too small.)

Materials such as paint and markers should always be nontoxic and washable. Always supervise your baby when he's using these, because even nontoxic varieties shouldn't be eaten.

Finding Games You Enjoy

Playing games with your baby should be a fun and enjoyable time for both of you. Just as you need to watch your baby's responses to see what she likes and dislikes, and to recognize when she's tired and through playing, you need to watch your own responses.

Some of the games will seem more natural and more fun to play and therefore more appealing than others. It's okay not to play the games you don't care for! No one's keeping score, and you don't get a Bad Parent of the Year Award just because you prefer not to play the "Guess Which Hand Game" in Chapter 8.

But we do suggest that you give the game a chance before you decide never to play it. Ask yourself if there's a way the game could be modified to make it more enjoyable for you. If you absolutely, positively, 100 percent don't want to sing, that's okay. Modify the game so that you talk to your baby instead of singing to him. We're not looking (or listening).

Try out some of the games at different times. You may find that a game is more interesting to you when your baby's older and more competent at playing it. Or you may find that a game makes you feel too silly and you just can't play it.

Don't force yourself to play when you don't feel like it or to play games that you don't enjoy. Your baby will sense your dislike of the activity and will think it has something to do with her. That's the last thing you want her to think, so do yourself and your baby a favor and play when you're energized and interested in the game.

Learning the Limits of Play

We can't think of a better way to spend your time than playing with your baby, but we do recognize that there are limits to play. No baby wants to be constantly "on" every moment he's awake. Nor is that good for his brain—it needs down time, too.

Dr. Larry's Little Known Facts

Your sleeping baby may look like he's not doing anything, but his brain is still humming along. Research shows that parts of his brain are actually more active while he's asleep than when he's awake. During sleep, your baby's brain takes a few moments to consolidate all the learning he's done and store some information in his memory. Many of those vital connections and pathways in your baby's brain (see Chapter 1) are actually made while he sleeps!

We also know that structured play is not the only way that your baby will learn and develop her brain. She needs the experience of screaming in a restaurant and being brought home to show her about limits and appropriate behavior; she needs to hang out and do nothing sometimes; and she needs plenty of sleep time so that her brain can get busy with its wiring.

Allowing Unstructured Freedom to Learn

In addition to letting your baby get some shut-eye, another way you can help her brain fire up is to give her plenty of opportunities for unstructured play. As she gets older, this unstructured time allows her to work things out for herself, experience alone time and learn to enjoy it, engage in imaginative and pretend play, and otherwise explore her creativity.

Though your baby is just a baby and isn't quite at the stage where she's playing with dolls and making up stories about what happened to them, here are ways you can encourage your baby's unstructured play:

- Let him explore a new environment (keeping an eye out for hazards) without guiding or intervening in his efforts.

- Put her on the floor with a toy and let her explore it with all her senses while you do something else, like put away the groceries.

- Simply watch what he does without feeling you have to join in or show him what to do.

By giving your baby opportunities to sort things out for herself, you'll help her build cognitive skills, such as problem solving, as well as self-help skills and creativity, not to mention confidence in her ability to entertain herself.

Considering Your Baby's Developmental Readiness

To be more successful with the games and activities we describe in this book, don't just look at the age suggested for each one. Consider as well your baby's developmental readiness for the game described.

Every baby is different. Your three-month-old may have the necessary skills to play some of the games designated for three months and up, but not for others. That's to be expected. If she's more of a verbal baby than an active one, she'll be more successful with the games in Chapter 4 than the games in Chapter 20.

That doesn't mean there's anything wrong with his development or that he "should" be able to play a game with a suggested age of three months and up. These are just general suggestions for possible times to try introducing the game to your baby.

As you read through the games and think about how you'll play them with your baby, spend some time considering her developmental readiness before springing into action. You'll save yourself some headaches!

The Least You Need to Know

- Bonding with your baby is an ongoing process—and not just one that involves one parent. You can use games to help everyone in the family bond with your baby.

- Trust your instincts when it comes to playing with your baby.

- Your baby looks to you for model behavior; you can show her how to play.

- You need to take steps to keep play safe and fun for your baby— and for you.

- Play has its limits; babies need unstructured time to just hang out, too.

Part 2

Teaching Your Baby Language

Language is a complex skill for your baby to master. Not only does he have to realize that the sounds you're making correspond with objects, actions, and ideas, but he has to learn how to imitate you in order to communicate his needs.

In this part, we'll give you plenty of games and activities you can play with your baby to help him understand the words you're saying, encourage him to communicate with you, and help him become more aware of himself and his relationship to the world around him.

4

Making Sense of Words and Objects

In This Chapter

- ◆ Communicating with your baby, and her with you
- ◆ Teaching common nouns, such as animal names and body parts
- ◆ Giving simple directions your baby can understand
- ◆ Stimulating language development with books and songs

The most important "game" you can play with your baby to encourage language development is, quite simply, to just talk to him. This will be easy for some moms and dads, but for those of us with a quieter nature, talking all the time may seem a little uncomfortable and awkward at first. But not to worry; over time, you'll be amazed at how you become more comfortable with talking to your baby. All you really have to remember is: if you think it, say it out loud.

Your baby loves to hear your voice, and this is not only how she learns language, but it is also an important part of how she will bond with you. Even at a month old, babies can distinguish their parents' voices from the voices of other adults, and they will turn or smile when they hear you speak.

In this chapter, we show you some tried-and-true methods of helping your baby learn to understand and respond to language. The games in this part of the book are designed to stimulate the "give and take" of your conversations with your baby. As you develop this give and take rhythm, you'll soon find that you come to intuitively know what kind of things interest your baby and at what times, such as when he feels like playing and when he wants to be quiet.

Conversations with Your Baby

When you talk to your baby, remember that people don't just use words to communicate. We also use facial expressions, tones of voice, gestures, and touch to say what we mean. Your baby will watch your face closely as you talk, studying your expression and watching your mouth and eyes. Hold your baby close when you talk so that she can see as well as hear what you're saying. Babies respond well to parentese, which will probably come quite naturally to you.

Remember that conversation with you baby is a two-way street. Notice your baby's expressions and recognize how she responds to you. Watching her face, as well as her body movements, will tell you what she enjoys, what she finds uninteresting, and even what bothers her. Also, give her a chance to take her turn in the conversation by pausing at appropriate places.

Use Your Baby's Name

When you talk with your baby throughout the day, use his name as much as possible. Replace "you" and "baby" with your baby's proper name. For instance, "Dylan and Daddy are going for a walk. Daddy likes to go for walks with Dylan." This helps your baby learn to identify his name, and it encourages your baby's self-awareness. It may seem odd at first, but after a while it will become natural ... so natural you might do this with other members of your household!

Use Nouns, not Pronouns

If you listen to an ordinary adult conversation, you'll hear a lot of references to "it," "them," "he," and "she." Adults generally don't have trouble following and connecting such pronoun references, but your baby needs to learn the specific names of objects and people you talk about. So when you speak to your baby, substitute nouns for pronouns as much as possible. For example, "Mama is changing Michelle's diaper. Michelle's diaper is very wet. No wonder Michelle is fussy!"

Repeat Yourself Over and Over ... and Over

Babies learn through repetition. They need to hear a word many times before they're able to reproduce it. When you talk with your baby, don't be afraid to say the same thing more than once, or in more than one way. This repetition helps your baby develop his language skills. For example, you might say, "Matthew is looking at the dog. Look at the dog. See what the dog is doing? What is the dog doing? Matthew likes looking at the dog." Over time, this repetition becomes a very natural habit—much to the annoyance of your adult friends. But it's good for your baby, and that's what counts!

6-14 The Naming Game
months

One of the most basic games you should play with your baby is naming and pointing to things in the baby's environment, specifically people, toys, and other objects. This game helps your baby start to understand her surroundings and develop a sense of connection to them, and you. Older babies love to play pointing and naming games, and by 12 months most babies can point to dozens of things when you name them. Your baby won't be able to say the names herself quite yet, but she'll know more than you can keep track of.

How to Play

Get your baby's attention by calling her name. Once she responds, say, "This is Sarah" (your baby's name) while pointing to her. Then point to another person and say, "That is Daddy" (or someone else in the room). Also point to or hold up a favorite toy and say its name, such as "train." Hand the toy to the child and repeat the toy's name: "This is Sarah's train."

Where and When

This is a great game to play anywhere, because there are basic objects—and people—everywhere. This game can help focus the baby both at home and when you're out in other environments, such as in the waiting room at the doctor's office or at the grocery store.

The best time to engage her in the naming game is when your baby seems alert and interested in her surroundings.

What You Are Teaching

This game teaches your baby that people and objects are identified by particular names. It is one of the earliest introductions to language your baby will have.

What You Need

Start out by identifying everyday toys and objects, such as a ball, rattle, spoon, teddy bear, blanket, apple, etc. Build and expand the range of toys, objects, and people as your baby learns them. Remember, repetition is key.

3+ months Say Then Do Game

One way to keep a conversation going with your child is to tell him what you're planning to do before you do it. As he gets older, these cues will help him prepare for transitions.

How to Play

As you go through your daily routine with your baby, tell him what you're planning to do before you do it. "Mommy is going to fix lunch." Then bring your baby to the kitchen as you prepare lunch. "Daddy is going to change Sam's diaper." Then bring the baby to the changing table.

Where and When

You can be anywhere to play this game, keeping in mind to communicate simple actions you plan to do and then do them. This game can be played anytime, especially when you're having one-on-one time with your baby.

What You Are Teaching

In this simple game, you are corresponding words to actions and communicating intentions. Your baby is learning how to associate words and intentions with his corresponding action.

What You Need

You don't need anything special for this game. It works best when you are executing basic, repetitive, everyday actions, such as opening the refrigerator or putting toys away.

 Act While You Speak Game

Because babies learn from non-verbal cues, you can reinforce what you're saying by using gestures and body language. This helps reduce your baby's frustration and helps her communicate when she sees how to show you what she wants. Some early childhood educators advocate using simple sign language to supplement spoken language, but you don't have to use an official sign language to help your baby "see" what you're saying.

How to Play

Use simple gestures to illustrate what you're saying. An obvious example is waving goodbye while saying, "Bye-bye." When it's time to eat, you may say, "Joanna sounds hungry! Time to eat," while putting your fingers to your mouth as if feeding yourself.

You can also act out the words to popular children's songs. Older babies love imitating your actions as you do this. If you sing a song about a bird, flap your arms like wings and encourage your child to do the same.

Where and When

You are always doing something, so it's easy to play this game anytime and anywhere. Think about your actions and speak about them as you do them.

What You Are Teaching

This game teaches your baby how gestures can communicate needs as well as words.

What You Need

Nothing special is needed for this game. Again, it's just a matter of consciously using body language and gestures combined with words to communicate with your baby.

3+ months Use One-Word Cues Game

Using short sentences helps you keep your baby's attention. But your baby's receptive language is far greater than his expressive language for the first several years, so also giving him one-word cues to use helps him learn to communicate effectively with you.

How to Play

Describe what you're doing with your baby in a simple sentence: "I'm picking Michael up." Then give a one-word cue that describes the action: "Up." To reinforce it, you may rephrase the sentence again: "Michael wants up." Eventually, your baby will focus in on the word "up" and use it to indicate when he wants to be picked up.

Where and When

This is another easy game to do anytime and anywhere; remember to condense what you say or what you do to one word.

What You Are Teaching

This is teaching your baby one-word commands that he can eventually use to communicate with you.

What You Need

You only need to remember to use one-word cues as you move about throughout your day with your baby.

Old Rhyme, New Word Game

Babies learn through repetition, and repetition is actually how they also notice something new. By changing the words in a rhyme your baby is familiar with, you can encourage her language memory skills.

How to Play

Repeat a rhyme or lullaby to your baby several times. Once your baby is familiar with the rhyme, change one of the words (a noun works best) to something nonsensical. Your baby will notice and possibly respond to the change. Older babies may think your "mistake" is funny.

Where and When

This game can be played anywhere at any time. Two good places for reciting rhymes are at home while reading and while driving in the car.

What You Are Teaching

This game teaches your baby to notice changes in familiar patterns.

 What You Need

You'll need books and CDs to learn rhymes so you can add little changes to the words once your baby learns them.

Tell a Story About Your Baby Game

Babies are extremely self-centered creatures, so they will pay attention to a story starring them. Your baby likes nothing more than hearing a story about himself … and you will find this to be true for many years to come. Telling stories to your baby about himself is great way to engage him.

How to Play

Spend a few minutes telling your baby about himself and the things that he does. Describe what he looks like, how strong he is, what his favorite toys are, and what he did today. You can say things like, "Tommy has brown hair" and "Tommy likes to play with his cars and trucks."

Where and When

This is a good game to play at home and out and about as you both discover more things he likes to see and do.

What You Are Teaching

This game shows your baby what words describe him and the world around him.

What You Need

You just need uninterrupted time throughout the day to talk to your baby.

6+ months Baby's Eavesdropping Game

Babies recognize their own names by about six months, and they will notice it being spoken even in adult-level conversations. Because babies pick up language skills even when the words are not directed at them, you'll want to expose your child to many listening opportunities. Hearing her name encourages your baby to pay attention to what you're saying, even if you're not speaking to her.

How to Play

Strike up a conversation about your baby with another adult, so your baby can hear it. Be sure to use your baby's name frequently as you speak.

Where and When

Play this game when other adults are present.

What You Are Teaching

This game teaches your baby listening skills.

What You Need

You just need other people to talk with and your baby sitting close by.

 # That's Not Daddy Game

Older babies enjoy hide-and-seek games, and this one encourages them to build their language skills as they play.

 How to Play

Have Daddy or another loved one hide someplace easy for your baby to spot. Bring your baby around the house looking for Daddy (or whoever is hiding). Point to the sofa and say, "That's not Daddy!" Look behind the door and say, "That's not Daddy." Repeat a few times until you find Daddy, then announce, "There's Daddy!"

 Where and When

This game is best played at home when Daddy or another caregiver is present.

 What You Are Teaching

You baby will begin to understand negatives and how to label people and objects.

 What You Need

A familiar loved one like Daddy or a grandparent is all you need.

 # Can You Do What I Say Game

Encouraging your child to show you that she understands your words builds her confidence—and yours!

 How to Play

Get your baby's attention by saying her name. Then direct her attention to the task that you want her to do. For example, you might say, "Danielle, your book is on the floor." Once her attention is on the book, give her the direction you want her to follow:

"Danielle, put your book away." Repeat the direction a few times. If she doesn't seem to understand, help her pick up the book and put it away, then say, "Danielle put her book away."

Where and When

Playing this game at home first with familiar objects works best, then you can work your way into doing this in other places to introduce more variety. This game can be played at different times of the day when you do something routinely, such as pick up toys or set the dinner table.

What You Are Teaching

This game teaches your baby to follow simple directions and demonstrates receptive language skills.

What You Need

You just need some simple tasks that your baby can perform.

3+ months Sing It Different Ways Game

Babies respond to singing voices. As we said earlier, babies learn through repetition, but they also pay attention to novelty. By varying the way you sing songs, you'll keep your baby's attention while reinforcing the words you're singing.

How to Play

Sing your baby's favorite song using different inflections: fast and high; low and slow; spoken and sing-songy. Notice how your baby reacts to the different ways you sing the song.

Where and When

This is good game to play while giving your baby a bath, driving in the car, doing small chores around the house, and anytime you can sing to your baby.

What You Are Teaching

Your baby is learning language development skills with this game.

What You Need

You just need the confidence to sing to your baby. Don't worry if you think you can't sing, because no matter what your voice sounds like, your baby likes it and needs to hear it.

 # Sing What You're Doing Game

Because babies naturally love to hear their loved ones sing, try singing in place of speaking to your baby. Even if your voice won't sell many concert tickets, do your baby a favor and sing anyway!

 How to Play

Instead of just telling your baby what you're doing throughout the day, sing it! Just add a tune to a sentence like "Mommy is changing Michael's diaper." Simply make up rhymes or songs that tell what you're doing as you're doing it.

 Where and When

This is a game that works anytime and anywhere, but if you're shy, you may want to reserve it for the privacy of your own home or car!

 What You Are Teaching

Through the use of song, this game teaches that words correspond with actions.

 What You Need

Again, all you need are just the guts to sing it instead of say it.

 # Where's This Game

Reading helps even young babies learn language skills. By playing reading games, you'll stimulate your baby's brain beyond her just hearing the words on a page.

How to Play

While young babies may be more interested in eating the book than looking at it, encourage your child to explore the world of books by picking out objects on the page. Ask your baby to find different objects. For example, "Where's the doggie?" and then show your baby where the doggy is on the page. Do this for several objects on the page. Eventually she will point to them on her own.

Where and When

This game works best in a comfy chair in a quiet place in your house.

What You Are Teaching

Your baby is learning the names of objects and is becoming familiar with books and reading.

What You Need

For this game, you need baby-friendly board books. They will contain objects and words appropriate for the age and this type of learning.

10+ months What It's Like Game

In order to express himself fully, your baby needs to learn more than just simple nouns and verbs, so this game encourages you and your baby to explore more descriptive language.

How to Play

Show your baby a favorite object, such as a stuffed animal. Tell your baby about it, using gestures when appropriate and encouraging him to manipulate the object as you describe it. "This is your stuffed bear. Look at his brown eyes [pointing to eyes]. See how his legs wiggle? [moving his legs] Feel how soft his fur is [place baby's hand on animal's fur]. What a soft bear."

Where and When

Play this game at home or outside when your baby is interested and engaged with a particular toy.

What You Are Teaching

This game teaches characteristics of named objects and descriptive language.

 What You Need

Your baby's favorite things are all you need for this game.

The Importance of Reading

The more you read to your baby at an early age, the easier it will be for her to master basic reading skills. Studies have shown that reading to infants improves parent-child bonding as well.

Babies enjoy physically handling a book, including chewing on it. By eight or nine months, your baby will be able to see simple pictures in a book and point to things she recognizes. Reading to your baby seems to stimulate the language centers of the brain, imprinting a template for the rhythm and organization of language and even simple vocabulary.

Reading to your baby will be most successful when you pay attention to her non-verbal communication. Let your baby take the lead as you turn the pages, and don't be surprised if she wants to stop, do something else, and then start again.

It's fun to read a book with your baby on your lap, but you'll also want to read to your baby when she's lying down, before bedtime or naptime. By just listening to you read, particularly if you're reading a nursery rhyme or other book with rhythmic language, your baby will develop listening and encoding skills—the way the brain makes sense out of words.

There are literally hundreds of great board books for babies. Here are some of the classics and my favorites:

- *Pat the Bunny* by Dorothy Kunhardt (Golden Books, 2001)

- *Where Does Maisy Live?* by Lucy Cousins (Walker Books Ltd, 2000)

- *Brown Bear, Brown Bear, What Do You See?* by Bill Martin Jr. (Henry Holt and Co., 1992)

- *Where's Spot?* by Eric Hill (Puffin, 2003)

- *Guess How Much I Love You* by Sam McBratney (Candlewick, 1996)

- *The Very Hungry Caterpillar* by Eric Carle (Puffin Books, 1994)

- *The Runaway Bunny* by Margaret Wise Brown (HarperCollins, 2005)

- *Goodnight Moon* by Margaret Wise (HarperCollins, 2005)

- *The Little Engine That Could* by Watty Piper (Grosset & Dunlap, 1978)

- *The Rainbow Fish* by Marcus Pfister (North-South, 2004)

- *From Head to Toe* by Eric Carle (HarperFestival, 1999)

- *Polar Bear, Polar Bear, What Do You Hear?* by Bill Martin Jr. (Henry Holt and Co., 1997)

- *The Wheels on the Bus* by Paul O. Zelinsky (Grosset & Dunlap, 1991)

The Least You Need to Know

- Talk out loud when you are around your baby. Name all the things you are doing and the things you see.

- Talk to your baby in the sing-songy manner that we used to call baby-talk, now called parentese.

- Watch your baby just as carefully as she watches you. Remember, your non-verbal communication is even more important than your words.

- Sing and read to your baby at every opportunity.

Encouraging Your Baby to Speak

Your baby's expressive language takes longer to develop than his receptive language (see Chapter 4), and he probably won't say his first recognizable word until about 12 months, but you can encourage his vocalizations from the very beginning.

In this chapter, we show you games to help your baby develop the oral skills needed to form words and understand the basic rules of conversation, such as taking turns.

Blowing Game

Helping your baby learn to manipulate her mouth, lips, and tongue makes it easier for her to learn to speak.

How to Play

Demonstrate blowing your breath out and encourage your baby to imitate you. Blow onto her hand or cheek so she can feel the air coming out of your mouth (stop if this seems to bother her). Tell her the story of *The Three Little Pigs*, and "huff and puff" to show her how to blow.

Then blow on a pinwheel to make it spin. Encourage her to blow on the pinwheel, too. Or you can show her how to blow bubbles. (Hold the bubble wand for her—and don't let her put it in her mouth.) You can also blow the bubbles already formed and see them move through the air. Or show her how to blow through a straw. (Don't let her play with the straw without your supervision.) All of these variations help her learn to control her lips, mouth, and tongue.

Where and When

This is a great game to play at a park or outside in your yard during the day.

What You Are Teaching

Your baby is learning oral skills needed to make words.

What You Need

You need a simple pinwheel, a jar of bubbles with a bubble wand, or a straw. Do not use chewing gum to blow bubbles, because babies are too young for it.

Repeating Babbles Game

Small babies make plenty of different sounds and they love interacting with their caregivers, so combining both activities together makes this game fun and educational for the baby—and parent.

How to Play

When your baby makes a noise—a gurgle or a coo or even a grunt—imitate these sounds. See how he responds, and take turns gurgling and cooing at each other.

Where and When

Anywhere is suitable for this game, and the best time to play is when your baby is alert and babbling.

What You Are Teaching

Your baby is learning that people will respond to his attempts at communication, thus encouraging further attempts.

What You Need

All you need is to be able to imitate the cooing and babbling sounds your baby makes.

Brainy Baby

Babbling with your baby encourages him to communicate, and he enjoys hearing you repeat his pretend talking. Most of the time, you will speak to him in normal words, which will help him build his vocabulary.

3-6 months Changing Babbles Game

By changing or adding to your baby's babbles, you can encourage her to attempt more complex sounds and to imitate you.

How to Play

When your baby is babbling, repeat the sounds she makes, but change them a little bit. Add another syllable or stretch out the vowel sound. You don't have to turn them into real words—nonsensical sounds work just fine for this game.

Where and When

Anywhere is fine to play this game, when your baby is alert and babbling.

What You Are Teaching

Your baby is learning listening and imitating skills that are important for language acquisition.

What You Need

All you need to is to add extra sounds on the end of your cooing and babbling.

 Recognizing First Words Game

As your baby babbles, sometimes he'll accidentally stumble on a combination of sounds that resemble a real word. At other times, he'll be trying to say a real word, but not clearly. If you listen closely, you'll be able to hear his words. By encouraging those sounds that do resemble real words, you'll help your baby develop an understanding of how communication works.

 How to Play

Listen carefully as your baby babbles. When he utters something that sounds like a real word, praise him and say, "Mama! [or whatever the word is] That's right. This is Mama." Use the word a few times, smiling and interacting with your baby as you do. This will help reinforce that certain sounds have meaning. You can play this game whether he stumbled on the sound accidentally or used it purposefully.

 Where and When

This game can certainly be played anytime, anywhere, because you never know when he'll say her first words.

 What You Are Teaching

You are letting your baby know that certain sounds have meaning.

 What You Need

All you need is to be listening to your baby's sounds.

 Making Mouth Noises Game

By letting your baby take the lead in communication, you can encourage her attempts to talk. This game also helps her develop control over her tongue, lips and mouth, which is necessary for her to form words.

How to Play

Encourage your baby to make sounds by clicking your tongue, blowing raspberries, or making kissing noises. Then let her respond and see what she does. Then try a different noise and see how she responds. Remember to take turns with your baby, and let her take the lead in the noisemaking if she wants.

Where and When

You can play this game anywhere and at any time.

What You Are Teaching

Your baby is learning to take turns and imitate, building the oral skills needed for conversation.

What You Need

All you need is to not be embarrassed about making noises with your mouth!

3-6+ months Singing Sound Effects Game

Babies love to hear you sing. In this game, you'll go a step beyond singing to him. You'll encourage him to imitate you and to make a variety of sounds.

How to Play

When you're singing to your baby, add sound effects to your song. Songs about animals of course lend themselves to "baa's" and "moo's"; use your imagination to add sound effects to any song. You might add a whistle to a song about a train, for example. Encourage your baby to imitate the sounds that you're making and be sure to give him a turn.

Where and When

The good times to play are at home or driving in the car, when he is awake and alert.

What You Are Teaching

You are teaching imitation skills necessary for language acquisition.

What You Need

All you need is the courage to sing and add new twists to songs here and there.

Brainy Baby

If your baby has siblings, encourage them to play these games with you and your baby. For example, small children will enjoy making animal noises to go along with "Old MacDonald Had a Farm." You can make playing these games a family time.

3-6+ months Asking Questions Game

Because young babies don't talk back, it can be easy for parents to fall into the habit of taking *at* them instead of *with* them—or not even talking with the baby at all. By inviting your baby to join the conversation, you'll help her develop good communication skills.

How to Play

As you go about your daily activities with your baby, ask questions about what your baby thinks, what she's doing, and how she feels. When you're changing her diaper, ask, "Is Jessica's diaper wet?" Wait for her answer (even though a young baby won't give one). Then make a statement that answers your question: "Jessica's diaper *is* wet." By answering the question, you're modeling possible responses for her.

Where and When

Play this game wherever and whenever you are doing something, particularly when it involves your baby.

What You Are Teaching

This game teaches your baby how to respond to others and take turns.

 ### What You Need

You don't need anything special; there are plenty of things to talk about in your daily routine.

 # 6-9+ months Embracing Invented Words Game

When your baby is young, you'll want to encourage his efforts at communication, no matter how awkward it is, instead of correcting his errors. Later, as your baby becomes a toddler and a preschooler, you can use the correct pronunciation of a word in your conversations with him.

 ### How to Play

When babies begin using words, they often use invented words or words that are only an approximation of the "real" word. For example, a baby might say "uh-uh" for "up," or "bah-bah" for blanket. Don't feel you have to correct your baby—at this stage, such corrections aren't helpful and may even discourage him. Go ahead and use the invented word in your response to him. "Here's Devon's bah-bah." Your baby will feel successful in communicating with you, which will encourage his further attempts.

 ### Where and When

Anywhere is appropriate for this game, and the best time is when he is trying to form words and using words he has already "invented."

 ### What You Are Teaching

In this game, you are showing your baby that you understand and appreciate his attempts at expressing himself.

 ### What You Need

You only need the words your baby has created to play this game.

You Say, I Say Game

9-12+ months

Encouraging your baby to imitate your words helps her master language skills. Basic conversational skills develop as she takes turns with you.

 ### How to Play

Take your baby for a walk around the house (or any other interesting location). Point to an object and name it. Then encourage your baby to say the name. Then move to the next object and do the same. If your baby shows a special interest in a certain object, examine it more closely, using descriptive words and encouraging her to do the same. If it's child-safe, let the child handle the object as you describe it. For example, if she shows interest in a ball when you point it out, say, "This ball is red. Red. Can Dina say red?" Then wait for her to respond before continuing.

 ### Where and When

Around the house or any other favorite location works for this game, and anytime works as long as your baby is alert and engaged.

 ### What You Are Teaching

This game teaches your baby imitation skills, names of objects, and turn-taking.

 ### What You Need

All you need is an environment with objects or people in it that your baby can easily name.

Tracking Words Baby Knows Game

12+ months

It may seem to take a long time for your baby to say his first words, but pretty soon he'll be saying plenty of them. Tracking his progress helps you, and him, see his development and growth.

How to Play

When your baby first begins using recognizable words, tape or tack a piece of cardboard or poster board to the wall of his room or in a readily accessible location, like the kitchen. Write the baby's age and the word he's using. As he continues adding to his vocabulary, note the words and when he first used them in conversation with you on the chart. You'll see his progress with this visual record, and so will he. You can share the information with his caregivers and have them encourage him to use the words you know that he can say.

Where and When

This is a game to do at home. Add to the chart anytime he uses a new word.

What You Are Teaching

You are showing your baby his progress and your recognition and appreciation of his attempts at communication.

What You Need

All you need is paper, cardboard or poster board, and something to write with.

Dr. Larry's Little Known Facts

Researchers say that how much a parent talks to his child greatly influences the child's vocabulary growth—both in the number of words a child knows and in how quickly he acquires those words. One study showed that children from disadvantaged backgrounds hear 32 million fewer words by age 5 than children from more advantaged backgrounds. So talk up a storm! It can only help your baby.

9-12+ months **Picking Up Game**

By taking turns picking up a toy or other object, you demonstrate the give-and-take of conversation to your baby. Plus, older babies love feeling helpful, and this game can turn into a helping game, where your baby brings you an object you need.

How to Play

Put your baby's favorite toy on a table, then take a few steps away from it. Say, "I'm going to pick up your toy." Then pick up the toy. Put it down again, then return to your original position. Ask your baby, "Please pick up your toy." If your baby doesn't understand the game at first, go with her to pick up the toy and try again. As your baby begins to understand your commands, she'll be able to pick up an object without your having to model the behavior first.

Where and When

Play this game at home or in a familiar environment when your baby is feeling active.

What You Are Teaching

This game helps your baby learn basic commands, imitation, and turn-taking.

What You Need

This game requires toys or other familiar objects that can be easily picked up by your baby.

9-12+ months Copycat Game

Babies learn much of their language through imitation. By playing the copycat game, you can encourage your baby to understand and develop more language skills.

How to Play

Sit with your baby in front of a mirror or face-to-face. Make a silly face (most babies love silly faces). Tell him, "You try." Once your baby is doing what you're doing, move on to other actions, such as touching your nose or touching your toes. This is a great game to play with other siblings, if your baby has any; most children know the game "Simon Says," and this is a simpler variation of that game.

Where and When

You can play this game anywhere; you can sit comfortably in front of a mirror or face-to-face when your baby is feeling energetic.

What You Are Teaching

Your baby is learning imitation skills and the connection between words and actions.

What You Need

A mirror of sufficient size to sit in front of together is ideal for this game.

9+ months Telephone Game

Your baby has probably seen you talk on the phone countless times. She will enjoy imitating what she thinks you say and do when you're on the phone.

How to Play

Give your baby one phone while you use the other. Take turns talking (or babbling) to each other. As you play, your baby will begin to imitate you and learn the turn-taking rules of conversation. By pretending to speak on the phone with your baby, you encourage her communication skills.

Where and When

This game is best played at home when your baby is alert and talkative.

What You Are Teaching

This is another game that teaches imitation, which encourages language acquisition. It also provides a forum in which to practice conversations, which encourages turn-taking and listening skills.

What You Need

Two play telephones *or* two telephones not in operation is all you need. This can include cell phones not turned on, but still be sure to supervise your baby.

 **Taping Baby Sounds Game**

Babies are fascinated by hearing themselves talk and by listening to conversations (real or babbled) with their loved ones.

How to Play

Record your baby when he is being particularly vocal. Or record a back-and-forth conversation between you and your baby (or another loved one and your baby). Play the recorded sounds back and watch your baby's reactions. It may stimulate him to say even more words, or he may be quiet and listen. Either response is helpful in encouraging your baby's further exploration of language and communication.

Where and When

Play this game at home or in a familiar environment when your baby is actively babbling or talking.

What You Are Teaching

This game is providing your baby feedback on his communication skills, because he can actually hear himself talk.

What You Need

This game requires a recorder—either a cassette tape or digital voice recorder.

 **Brainy Baby**

If your baby likes to hear the sound of his voice, you may want to consider investing in a child-safe tape recorder that he can manipulate and learn to use himself (under your supervision, of course).

 **What Do You Want Game**

If you overanticipate your baby's needs, you can squelch her attempts at communicating. By giving your baby tools to help communicate, you encourage her efforts.

How to Play

When your baby points or reaches for her favorite toy, instead of handing it to her, ask her what she wants. Give her a couple options and encourage her to tell you which one. "Does Beth want the cup? [showing her the cup] or does Beth want the doll? [showing her the doll]." You can also do this with her other cues. For example, if she fusses and you know it's her I-need-my-diaper-changed fuss, instead of just changing her, ask her to tell you what she needs. "Is Beth's diaper wet? Does Beth want a clean diaper?" Encourage her to respond.

Where and When

This game is especially good anytime and anywhere, because babies always want or need something.

What You Are Teaching

This game teaches your baby that words can, and should, be used to communicate with caregivers.

What You Need

All you need for this game is patience and the forethought not to always simply execute what you know your baby wants.

 Taking Turns Game

A basic conversational skill is taking turns. Showing your baby how to take turns helps him understand the fundamentals of communicating with others.

How to Play

Emphasize phrases used in turn-taking as you go about your daily activities with your baby. At the grocery store, you can explain, "We're waiting in line for our turn. When it's our turn, we can pay for the groceries."

Set up opportunities to explore turn-taking throughout the day. For example, you might wash your baby's face and then say, "It's my turn," and wash your own face. Do the same when it's time to put on coats and hats before going outside. Look for turn-taking opportunities everywhere.

Where and When

Turn-taking is ever present throughout the day, so this game can really be played anytime and anywhere you encounter these opportunities.

What You Are Teaching

This game shows your baby how to take turns and teaches basic communication skills.

What You Need

Turn-taking occasions are all you need to play this game. Remember to create some, too.

The Least You Need to Know

◆ Your baby's ability to manipulate his tongue, lips, and mouth (oral skills) is crucial to learning to talk.

◆ Engaging your baby in conversations—whether babbles or real words—encourages her attempts to communicate.

◆ Recognizing and encouraging your baby's attempts at talking will help him develop his skills.

◆ Imitating others is an important way that babies learn to talk.

◆ Teaching turn-taking will help your baby learn basic conversational skills.

6

Teaching Your Baby About Himself/Herself

In This Chapter

◆ Describing your baby's body parts so she can begin to recognize them

◆ Playing games that encourage your baby's self-awareness

◆ Helping your baby learn about himself in relationship to his environment

◆ Showing your baby how she is a separate person from you and her other loved ones

It's your responsibility to help your baby understand himself as an independent person from you and to encourage him to begin to develop his own identity. In this chapter, we provide some games give him information about himself, and others that show him about how he fits into the world around him. Still others help him learn to manipulate his body in the environment around him. All of the games are intended to help your baby learn about himself.

3-6+ months Label Body Parts Game

As your baby begins to be more aware of the world around her, she'll explore how her body works. Giving her the words for her body parts helps her to recognize them—then someday she'll be able to name them herself.

How to Play

When your baby is moving about, gaining control over her body, spend a few minutes touching her major body parts and telling her what they're called. For example, touch her arm and say, "This is Chantelle's arm." Touch her nose and say, "This is Chantelle's nose." As you're dressing her, say, "Mama puts Chantelle's foot in the sock. This is Chantelle's foot."

Where and When

Playing this game is easily done at home, particularly when getting dressed and when your baby is alert and moving about.

What You Are Teaching

This game teaches your baby body awareness and the names of different body parts.

What You Need

You just need your bodies to play this game, and baby books showing people also work well, so you can point to and identify different body parts.

3-6+ months Look in the Mirror Game

To encourage your baby's self-awareness, give him the opportunity to look in the mirror. It's not vanity—it's education!

How to Play

Sit with your baby on your lap in front of a mirror so he can see his face. Point out his features in the mirror. "Those are Andre's eyes. There's Andre's nose." Comment on his facial expression. "Andre is smiling. See Andre's mouth smile? Andre must be happy."

Where and When

This game is best played at home when your baby is alert and attentive.

What You Are Teaching

You are showing and teaching your baby what he looks like, the names of his body parts, and what his facial expressions mean.

What You Need

All you need for this game is a mirror big enough so you can easily see each other.

Dr. Larry's Little Known Facts

Your baby won't realize that it's *him* in the mirror until he's about 15 months old, because it takes a while for him to develop the necessary self-awareness and self-identification. But he'll be interested in the face in the mirror long before he recognizes himself.

 Name Baby's Clothing Game

Talking with your baby as you give her personal care helps her develop a fuller awareness of herself and her immediate surroundings.

How to Play

As you dress your baby, lift up each piece of clothing and show it to her. Say, "Here is Megan's shirt. Touch Megan's shirt." Let her touch the shirt, or help her touch the shirt. Then tell her, "Time to put on Megan's shirt." Do this with different pieces of her clothing, naming each one.

Where and When

Play this game at home in the morning when you're dressing your baby for the day.

What You Are Teaching

This game teaches your baby body awareness and the names of objects.

What You Need

Your baby's usual clothing is all you need.

 What Baby Likes Game

Your baby has definite preferences about what he eats and what he does—not to mention who he does it with. Talking about his preferences helps him actually learn about himself.

How to Play

As you go through your daily activities with your baby, talk about what he likes and doesn't like. If a loud noise startles him, say, "Damon does not like loud noises!" If he's offered a favorite toy, say, "Damon likes his toy car." You can also talk about what *you* like and don't like, so that he can see that other people have different likes and dislikes. For example, you may say, "Damon likes to drop his food on the floor. Daddy doesn't like to clean it up."

Where and When

Play this game anytime at home or when you're out and about having different experiences.

What You Are Teaching

Your baby is learning self-awareness and differences between people.

What You Need

Your daily routine and activities are all you need to point out likes and dislikes to your baby.

What Baby Does Game

Describing your baby's activities as she does them helps her understand her effect on the world around her.

How to Play

Throughout the day, talk with your baby about what she's done—and how she felt about it. For example, at lunchtime, you can say, "It's lunchtime already! What a busy day. First, Monique woke up and Mama changed her diaper. Then Daddy gave Monique breakfast. Monique liked having Daddy give her breakfast" and so on, describing the day up until lunchtime. At another interval later in the day, like at dinnertime or bedtime, you can bring the day's summary up to date. Doing this a few times a day helps your baby learn to organize her experiences and begin to anticipate routine events and activities.

Where and When

You can play this game anywhere at convenient intervals throughout the day—at lunchtime, after naptime, and at bedtime.

What You Are Teaching

You baby starts to gain self-awareness and learn how her days are structured.

What You Need

You just need a good memory to play this game.

6-9+ months What Baby Does All Day Photo Game

Helping your baby visualize what his typical day looks like allows him to understand what's happening in his world and gives him a feeling of power and control.

How to Play

Over the course of several days, take photos of the everyday happenings that occur in your baby's life. For example, take a picture of him awake in his crib, a picture of Mommy kissing him goodbye before going to work, a picture of the interior of his day-care setting, a picture of him at the table eating a meal, and so on.

Put the pictures in a small photo album, labeling them with simple descriptions, such as "Wake-up time" and "Lunchtime." As you transition from one activity to another throughout the day, show the book to your baby and, pointing to the appropriate photos, say, "It was time for playing. Now it's time for lunch. Next it will be time for a nap."

 Where and When

The great thing about photos is you can take them with you and look at them anywhere. The best time to play this game is at *transition times* throughout the day.

What You Are Teaching

You baby is learning to anticipate what will happen in a given day.

What You Need

Materials needed are a camera (either digital or film), printed photos, a photo album, and sticky labels.

Transition times are periods throughout the day when your baby moves from one activity to another, such as from playing to napping. These can be stressful times for your baby, and the "What Baby Does All Day Photo Game" can help ease the stress of those changes.

0-6 months What's Baby's Name Game

Your baby will be able to recognize her own name at about four months of age, and research shows that she uses it as a marker to help her understand other words that you use when speaking, and singing, to her. So helping your child learn to recognize her name is crucial for her language development.

How to Play

Throughout the day as you interact with your child, in addition to speaking her name, also sing it in a song you make up. For instance, sing "What is baby's name? Baby's name is Michaela," and add lines that describe your baby. Always use your baby's name: "Michaela's eyes are blue. Michaela has a nice smile." If you can make the song rhyme, even better!

Where and When

Singing your baby's name can be done anywhere at any time (depending on how you feel about others hearing you sing!).

 What You Are Teaching

This game teaches your baby self-awareness.

What You Need

All you need is the courage to sing and make up a song.

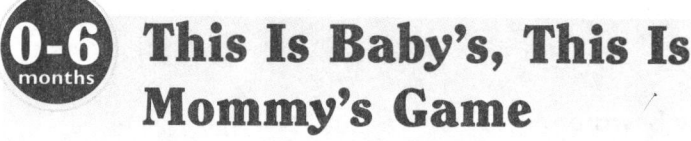 **0-6** months **This Is Baby's, This Is Mommy's Game**

Very young babies don't just think they're the center of the universe, they think they *are* the universe. One of their developmental stages is the ability to form a separate identity from the world, and the people, around them.

Your baby is likely to identify most strongly with his primary caregiver, so helping him understand that the primary caregiver is a separate person (but a loving and available one!) encourages your baby's self-awareness.

 How to Play

When your baby is awake in his crib, or when you're holding him in your arms, touch your nose and say, "This is Mommy's nose." Then touch your baby's nose and say, "This is Kevin's nose." Touch other parts of your body and your baby's. As your baby gets older, you can also identify belongings this way: "This is Mommy's book. That is Kevin's book."

Where and When

Play this game anywhere when you have your baby's attention.

What You Are Teaching

You baby is gaining self-awareness and learning to form identities.

What You Need

Nothing special is necessary for this game; just use your body and everyday objects around you.

 Handprint Game

Your baby will grow bigger much faster than you can believe, so it's fun to have a visual reminder of how small she once was. Plus, the experience of doing this activity makes your baby more aware of her hands. You can also make this a footprint game—or do both at the same time.

Baby Beware

Don't let your baby put her hands in her mouth when you do the Handprint Game. And remember to use nontoxic, easily washable paint.

How to Play

Using a small amount of nontoxic paint, brush a little on your baby's hand with your fingers (or a small paintbrush), starting at her fingers and working down her palm. Stamp her hand on paper or the surface you're applying the print to. Let it dry, then hang it on the wall or put it in a photo album to show to her later. Periodically do more handprints (or footprints) to show your baby's growth.

Where and When

Do this game at home or in an activity setting when she is alert and cooperative.

What You Are Teaching

Along with providing tactile stimulation and sentimental memories, this game teaches your baby both body part awareness and self-awareness.

What You Need

Materials for this game include cardboard, a T-shirt, construction paper or other surfaces to apply your baby's prints to, nontoxic paint, wipes, and a small paintbrush (if desired).

 # Where Is the Baby Game

This is a version of hide-and-seek that doesn't require your baby to be mobile, and may provoke some giggles when he realizes you're trying to find him.

 ### How to Play

This game is most fun if another adult or child joins in. While your baby is on the floor, being held by another person, or in another position to observe you, say, "Where is Jacques? I just saw him!" Look under the sofa, behind the wall hanging, out the window, and so on. Then be very surprised to find the baby. As he gets older, he may try to hide from you (turning this into a real game of hide-and-seek) or he may tell you where to find him.

 ### Where and When

Play this game anytime at home, because this is an environment your baby is familiar and comfortable with, and in time you can play it in other trusted places.

 ### What You Are Teaching

Your baby is learning awareness of self in relation to the outside world.

 ### What You Need

All you need is some furniture to look under and behind.

One for You, One for Me Game

As your baby learns about herself, she begins to see herself as a separate person, and taking turns helps reinforce her awareness of "me" and "you." This game is a simple and stress-free way to introduce this concept to your baby.

How to Play

Gather toys or a snack, such as crackers or cereal, and play this simple turn-taking game. Put one toy in front of your baby and say, "That is Jenny's." Put one in front of yourself and say, "This is Mommy's." Repeat until the toys or the snacks have been distributed and then enjoy playing or eating together.

Where and When

This game can be played at home during playtime or snacktime.

What You Are Teaching

Your baby is learning self-awareness, identity formation, and turn-taking skills.

What You Need

A collection of toys or a snack with pieces, such as crackers, is all you need.

> **Dr. Larry's Little Known Facts**
>
> Research shows that babies as young as three months old already understand how taking turns works in conversations. They find it harder to apply this concept to games and other activities. In fact, the ability to share toys, which is based on taking turns, won't come until your baby turns into a two- or three-year-old.

3+ months **This Little Piggy Game**

Babies learn a lot through their sense of touch. This game shows your baby something about his body by combining language with touch.

How to Play

Lightly squeeze your baby's toes with your fingers as you say the "This Little Piggy" rhyme. His response may be to kick, but that's just fine—you're showing him his body.

Where and When

Anyplace where your baby is barefoot works for this game.

What You Are Teaching

This game teaches self-awareness.

What You Need

A bare foot is all you need to play this game.

3-6 months Squeaky Toy Game

As your baby gains motor control over her body, she'll develop the ability to grasp objects. Encouraging her efforts helps her understand what her body is capable of doing.

How to Play

With your baby in her crib or held by another person, squeak a squeaky toy and offer it to her. She may just wiggle her arms and legs at first, but soon she'll reach for the toy and grasp it. When she's able to make it squeak herself, she'll have a proud feeling of accomplishment. The game helps her understand what her hands can do.

Where and When

Play this game at home anytime.

What You Are Teaching

This game shows your baby she can manipulate her environment and bring things to herself rather than waiting passively to receive them.

What You Need

A baby-appropriate toy that squeaks is all you need.

3-6 months Show Baby's Hands Game

Your baby discovers his hands at about three months of age. Encouraging him to use them and manipulate objects with them gives him a feeling of control over himself and his environment.

How to Play

Show your baby his hands at various times throughout the day. For example, when you're dressing him, you might put his arm through a sleeve and say, "Where is Mitchell's hand? Here is Mitchell's hand!" and show your baby his hand. Offer him a toy, saying, "Where is Mitchell's hand? Here it is." Then put the toy in his hand. He may not grasp it right away, but over time he will learn what you expect him to do.

Where and When

This game can be played anytime and anywhere, particularly when getting dressed or undressed.

What You Are Teaching

You are showing your baby that his hands are part of him and that they can be used to affect the environment.

What You Need

All you need are your baby's hands.

Birth + Rub Baby's Tummy Game

Using gentle touch can help you and your baby bond. This game is also about helping your baby understand and experience her body.

How to Play

With a light, gentle touch, stroke your baby's bare belly and say, "This is Tyra's tummy." Use a little lotion on your hands, if you and your baby like that. If your baby enjoys tickling, you can try that, too. Turn it into a game: "1, 2, 3 ... tickle!" Your baby will learn to anticipate the tickle, and that increases her enjoyment of the game.

Where and When

Play this game at home while dressing or after a bath.

What You Are Teaching

This game teaches your baby about self-awareness and loving touch.

What You Need

You don't need anything for this game, but baby lotion can add a little variety.

 **Dr. Larry's Little Known Facts**

Studies show that people—including babies—who laugh when you tickle them aren't doing it because they enjoy the feeling (they may not), but because they enjoy the interaction with you. A little tickling goes a long way, so don't overstimulate your baby. If she squirms or fusses or tries to scoot out of the way, stop.

6+ months **Where's Baby's Foot Photo Game**

As you know by now, babies enjoy looking at pictures, particularly of themselves. Though your baby won't recognize himself right away in pictures, you can use photos of your baby to teach him about himself.

 How to Play

Take a photo of your baby lying in his crib or on the floor so that you can capture him full length on film. If you have the option, blow the photo up on a color copier so that it's easier to see the details. (If you do this, slip the photocopied paper into a plastic sleeve so that your baby won't destroy it if he touches it.)

Show the photo to your baby and ask, "Where is Gavin's foot?" Touch the foot on the photo and say, "There is Gavin's foot." Continue asking questions and pointing out your baby's body parts.

 Where and When

This game is suitable anywhere and anytime your baby is alert and attentive.

 **What You Are Teaching**

This game teaches self-awareness along with the names of body parts.

What You Need

You need a camera—either digital or film—and the printed photos of your baby, ideally enlarged.

The Least You Need to Know

- Playing turn-taking games with your baby helps her see herself as a separate person from you.

- Helping your baby become familiar with his body encourages his self-awareness.

- Showing your baby how to use her body helps her become more independent and gives her a feeling of power and control.

- Naming and describing your baby to your baby, including his body parts and his immediate environment, helps him make sense of it all.

Teaching Your Baby to Think

We often think of learning as cramming facts into our brains so that we know *what* to think—and can regurgitate it for a teacher. But the most important skill you can teach your baby is *how* to think. Once your baby figures out how to use her brain to solve problems, look out!

In this part, we'll show you a variety of games and activities you can play with your baby to help her explore the world, develop her ability to remember experiences and words, and use her reasoning skills to figure out how to get what she wants.

Increasing Your Baby's Memory

In This Chapter

- ◆ Developing your baby's memory skills using different games and resources

- ◆ Teaching object permanence—a critical developmental stage

- ◆ Making games out of your routines and schedules

- ◆ Helping your baby learn to recall and tell stories in chronological order

Showing your baby how to flex her memory muscles helps her build her language skills—and other skills she'll need as she grows up, such as social and problem-solving skills.

In this chapter, you can find lots of games to help your baby learn to remember and recall details of her day and her family life. These games encourage her to recognize and remember important people, as well as stories about her life.

6+ months Where's the Spoon Game

This quick game with a spoon, or another familiar object, can be played at mealtime—or anytime. Try it a few times to see if your baby picks up on what you're doing. If not, wait a week or two and try again. Once she starts looking for the spoon, you can see her steady progress toward mastering the concept of *object permanence*.

BABY BABBLE

Object permanence refers to the understanding that an object continues to exist even if you don't see it. Your baby isn't born with this understanding, but acquires it over time. One of the reasons a young baby is upset when her caregiver leaves is that she doesn't understand that her caregiver will come back! For all that she knows, her caregiver has ceased to exist. Most babies learn object permanence at about eight months.

How to Play

When your baby has finished eating a meal, take the spoon that you fed your baby with and move it out of her direct line of sight. Ask "Where's the spoon?" and then show her the spoon. Gradually move the spoon behind your back, where she can't see it. Eventually she will learn to point to where the spoon is, even though she can't see it.

You can play the same game with a favorite toy, partially hiding it under a pillow at first. Later she'll be able to find it even if it's completely hidden, if you show her where you're hiding it. She'll be a little older (around two) before she can find it without seeing you hide it first.

Where and When

Play this game at home or wherever you may be after finishing a meal.

What You Are Teaching

Your baby learns object permanence while playing this type of game.

What You Need

You need a spoon or your baby's favorite toy or book to play this game.

3+ months Bedtime Ritual Game

Babies like ritual and repetition. They're happier and less stressed when days—and nights—follow a similar routine. You can create a bedtime ritual for your baby that is soothing and improves the likelihood of him going to bed with few complaints and sleeping well once he's there.

How to Play

Start by creating a bedtime routine with your baby. Based on your baby's habits, choose a specific bedtime. In the time leading up to the chosen hour, plan low-key activities such as taking a relaxing bath, reading a book, or rocking in a rocking chair. Then bring your baby to his room and tuck him in, singing a few lullabies or other songs he likes. An older baby may want a favorite stuffed animal or blanket to accompany him, and that's fine.

Once you've established the ritual, you can ask your older baby to remind you of the bedtime routine. "Sam has taken a bath. What's next before Sam goes night-night?" Your baby will learn to anticipate the routine, and find reassurance and comfort in it.

Where and When

At home at bedtime, as well as when sleeping in other places, to maintain the consistency as much as possible.

What You Are Teaching

Having rituals promotes memory skills and an understanding of what can be counted on day after day.

What You Need

Consistency and maintenance of routines and schedules are what you need to make this game most effective for your baby.

6+ months Where's My Hat Game

A variation of the "Where's the Spoon Game," this game enlists your baby's help in finding a missing (though visible) object—this time, it's one that belongs to you.

How to Play

Put one of your belongings, such as a hat, where your baby can see it. Ask your baby, "Where is my hat?" If your baby is mobile, she may walk over to it and bring it to you. If she's younger, encourage her to gesture toward the object. Carry her with you as you look. As your baby starts to understand the game better, make it harder to find the missing object. Part of the fun of this game is helping her find something that belongs to you (for once!).

Where and When

At home, anytime—preferably not when you're really missing something and needing to be somewhere soon!

What You Are Teaching

You baby is adding on to her object permanence skills through playing this game with items other than her own.

What You Need

A hat or other personal belonging your baby readily recognizes is what will grab her attention the most for this game.

6+ months Where Does This Go Game

Babies recognize more about their environment than we probably realize. They'll notice everything from misplaced objects to rearranged furniture. This game builds their memory of their immediate surroundings.

How to Play

Take an object from your baby's immediate surroundings. Show the object to him and ask, "Where does this go?" Encourage him to point or show you where. For younger babies, let him see you pick up the object and then give him a chance to respond to your question. Older babies will be able to tell you where the object goes even if they don't see where you picked it up.

Where and When

The best places to play are at home or another place your baby is familiar with. It's best during playtime, when you have time to let your baby take his time to respond and participate, as opposed to when you're in a rush to pick things up.

What You Are Teaching

Your baby acquires memory and communication skills for where objects belong in this game.

What You Need

Familiar surroundings and objects from your baby's room, playroom, or other familiar space are needed to play.

6+ months Favorite People Game

Babies love looking at pictures of people they know, and they enjoy hearing stories about them. A photo album of their loved ones helps them remember people they don't see regularly.

How to Play

Collect photographs of your baby's loved ones and put them in a photo album. You can play several games with your baby that will help her remember the important people in her life:

1. You can go through the photo album and name the people you see so that your baby begins to associate the names with the faces.

2. Show your baby the photo album before a loved one comes to visit, asking questions such as, "Do you know who is coming to visit?" Then point to the appropriate picture and say the person's name. Ask other questions to help prompt her memory of that person. "Do you remember when Nana took Gretchen to the park last week? Gretchen played in the sand."

3. For older babies, another game to play is to tell stories about the people in the pictures. Your baby will start to learn more about her family this way, too.

Where and When

Play this game at home, anytime. You can also take photo albums along in the car or stroller to have something to play with when you go out.

What You Are Teaching

Recognition and individualization of loved ones is what your baby is learning here.

 ## What You Need

One or two small photo albums, small enough that your baby could eventually hold them on her own, and photos of loved ones makes the game easy to play.

Dr. Larry's Little Known Facts

Even though your baby won't recognize a picture of herself until she's about 15 months old, she'll recognize a picture of her primary caregiver a lot earlier. One study showed that six-month-olds can recognize a photograph of their mother even when shown photographs of several different people at the same time.

 # 6+ months **Head, Nose, and Mouth Game**

Your baby's affinity for faces will make this game fun for him to play, even as it teaches him how to remember and show you what he recalls.

 ## How to Play

Once you've spent some time teaching your baby about his body parts (see Chapter 6, "Label Body Parts Game"), move on to this game. Instead of pointing out a body part and naming it, ask your baby, "Where is Nick's head?" Praise him when he points to it. If he doesn't, touch his head and say, "Here is Nick's head." Then ask, "Where is Mommy's head?" and wait for his response. Show him "This is Mommy's head" if he doesn't respond. Soon he will remember to point to his head, your head, and anyone else's head. Play this game while using your nose, mouth, and other parts of your head.

Where and When

Anywhere and anytime works for this fun game, because no special equipment is required!

What You Are Teaching

Your baby will have fun gaining memory skills and learning the names of body parts with this game.

What You Need

You just need your head!

 ## Who Says That Game

Many babies enjoy looking at pictures of animals and making animal sounds. This game combines both of these pleasures for an educational purpose.

How to Play

Show your baby pictures of animals and say the sound associated with each animal ("baa" for sheep, "moo" for cow, etc.). Then make an animal sound and ask, "Who says that?" Show her the pictures one at a time and ask, "Does a cow say that?" until you find the picture that matches the sound. She can also pick the picture she wants to talk about, and you can reverse the game. "Does the animal in this picture say 'moo'? Does this animal say 'baa'?" Encourage your baby to make the appropriate sound.

Where and When

At home or in any comfortable place where you and your baby can look at pictures together and play anytime your baby is willing.

What You Are Teaching

You are facilitating the learning of memory and matching skills for your baby in this game.

What You Need

Use simple pictures of farm animals in books, magazines, or on flashcards.

6+ months Counting Game

Though your baby will be older before he masters numbers, this game gets him off to a good start and gets you in the habit of counting objects with him.

How to Play

With your baby on your lap, count the fingers on his hands, then the toes on his feet. Show him your hand and count the fingers on your hand. Gather a group of toys together and count them, touching each toy as you count.

Where and When

Play in any comfortable spot, whether it's at home, in a coffee shop, or in a waiting room when your baby is contently sitting in your lap.

What You Are Teaching

Your baby is learning numbers and starting to pick up counting skills with this game.

What You Need

Simple objects to count, such as fingers, toes, pieces of cereal, or snacks.

Dr. Larry's Little Known Facts

In 1992, researcher Karen Wynn conducted a study that appeared to show that babies as young as five months old can demonstrate intuitive arithmetic skills, such as adding 1 + 1 or subtracting 2 − 1. Her research has led her to believe that babies have innate number skills, though other researchers think that perhaps the babies are using visual clues that help them judge "larger" and "smaller"—clues that may look like math but are non-numeric.

 Change the Ending Game

Babies need repetition to learn, and they enjoy hearing the same stories over and over. But adding something new and different to a story enhances their ability to learn by challenging them to remember the previous version.

How to Play

Your baby will listen, and want to listen, to the same story over and over again. Eventually she'll be able to tell the story word-for-word, or nearly so. By changing the ending of a favorite story, you'll surprise your baby and build her memory skills. She will know that something is different and will work to figure out what that is by comparing the new version of the story with the previous version she has in her memory.

Where and When

Anywhere you are reading or telling stories to your baby is appropriate for this game, whether it's during the day or reading before going to bed.

What You Are Teaching

The subtle differences you infuse into familiar stories in this game promote memory and change identification skills for your baby.

What You Need

Favorite stories and books and a little imagination are all you need to keep your baby's interest piqued.

Fill in the Action Game

Because your baby likes repetition, by the time he's a year or so old, he'll have memorized his favorite songs and stories. Challenge his memory—and build his anticipation and motor skills—with this game.

How to Play

Sing a few phrases of your baby's favorite song, adding an action at the end of a line. For example, if the "itsy-bitsy spider" crawls somewhere, imitate a crawling insect with your fingers. Encourage your baby to do the same.

Once your baby is doing the action with you, sing the line and wait for your baby to fill in the action. If he doesn't respond at first, show him the action, then try again a few lines later.

Where and When

This game is appropriate anyplace you are telling favorite stories or singing favorite songs.

What You Are Teaching

By not always providing the cue for your baby, you are helping promote his memory skills.

What You Need

Having your baby's favorite songs and stories memorized is all you need—which likely won't be hard, because you've heard them so many times!

 What's in the Treasure Box Game

Babies develop a fondness for certain toys and objects. You can use these toys to help your baby improve her memory. (See Chapter 9 for a related game, "Gathering Treasures Game," and Chapter 13 for another, "Create a Treasure Box Game.")

How to Play

While your baby watches, put her toys in a box, the "treasure" box. Take them out one by one, describing each one as you do so. "Here is Jayme's red truck. Here is Jayme's soft bunny." Then place a towel over the top of the box. Put your hand inside and take out one toy. Describe it before you pull it out of the box.

Then show your baby the toy. Encourage her to put her hand in the box. When she pulls the toy out, describe it to her. As she gets older, ask her to tell you what toy she has in her hand before she takes it out of the box.

Where and When

At home where your baby's toys are, anytime she's interested in playing with the treasure box.

What You Are Teaching

Putting familiar objects out of sight, then bringing them into view and describing what they are increases your baby's memory skills.

What You Need

This game is simple to assemble, because you likely already have everything you need: a box or some type of container large enough to fit toys in, a towel or piece of fabric to cover the box opening, and a collection of your baby's favorite toys or objects.

6+ months Jack-in-the-Box Game

You may remember playing with a jack-in-the-box when you were a child—turning the crank and anticipating when the jack would pop out. Despite the simplicity of the game, babies love to do it over and over.

How to Play

Sit with your child and turn the crank of a jack-in-the-box. Let him know what's coming: "Here comes the jack-in-the-box!" When it pops out, he may be surprised a time or two, but eventually he will catch on that it always pops out at a certain time. Soon he'll be anticipating its appearance.

If you don't have a jack-in-the-box, you can play a version of this game by singing "Pop Goes the Weasel" and using dramatic hand gestures to signal the pop. Soon your baby will be joining you in showing "pop!"

 ### Where and When

At home or anywhere you are out playing with your baby is suitable to play this game, like in a park or at a friend's house. You can play anytime during playtime, but close to bedtime or naptime may not be the best idea, because the game may get him excited and wound up.

What You Are Teaching

The fun of waiting for that "pop" teaches your baby to anticipate events and helps develop his memory skills.

What You Need

A jack-in-the-box toy is good for playing this game, because there's also the fun of turning the handle.

> **Brainy Baby**
>
> Encouraging your baby to turn the crank on the jack-in-the-box helps him develop eye-hand and hand-arm coordination (see Chapter 19). Like many of the games in this book, this game helps your baby develop more than one skill.

 ## 12+ months Find the Matching Card Game

This matching game grows as your child does, teaching her a number of different skills as she plays the game according to her ability.

How to Play

Place two or three pairs of cards on the floor, face up. Sitting with your baby, ask, "Where are the cows?" or whatever is appropriate to the set of cards. Pick up the matching cards and show them to your baby, then set them aside. Then ask her, "Where are the ducks?" or whatever is appropriate, until all the matches are made.

As your baby grows, you can add complexity to the game by spreading out more than two or three pairs at a time and more different images to match. When your baby is a preschooler, you can turn the cards over (face down) and play a turn-taking matching game where you try to remember where various matches are.

Where and When

At home or wherever you are having playtime is suitable for playing this game.

What You Are Teaching

This game teaches a variety of skills including matching, memory, sorting, and concentration.

What You Need

To play, have pairs of cards with simple designs handy. Pictures of animals work best at this age. You can even make them yourself by drawing pictures on cardstock or printing out clip art from your computer.

What Did Baby Do Today Game

Your baby likes to know what's going to happen before it happens, but he also likes to know what just happened, after it happened. You can help him learn to tell stories in a chronological way about what will or did happen with this game.

How to Play

As your baby is settling down for his bedtime routine, recount the events of the day with him. Start at the beginning and go through the highlights of the day. Be sure to use time marker words like "first," "next," "at lunchtime," and "after that." Another good time to play this game is at dinner when your family is gathered together. Everyone can tell about his or her day.

Where and When

You can play this game anywhere you are at the end of the day, whether it's at home or riding in the car, at dinnertime or bedtime.

 What You Are Teaching

Your baby is learning chronology and how to recall and retell events of the day.

What You Need

All you need is to recollect your day's events.

12+ months Draw Baby's Day Game

Older babies like to scribble with crayons and markers, and you can use this interest to help your baby remember and tell about her day.

How to Play

With your baby, draw a picture of the events that took place during the day, telling a story as you do so. For instance, you may say, "Erika woke up in her crib," and draw a picture of a crib. (You don't need to be an art expert—stick figures are fine!) Then say, "Mama and Erika had breakfast," and draw a bowl of cereal or a cup of milk. Encourage your baby to scribble with you as you draw.

Where and When

At home or anywhere you are in mid- to late day is suitable to play this game.

What You Are Teaching

This game teaches your baby the skill of remembering and recalling events and the telling stories in chronological order.

What You Need

Materials you need are crayons or nontoxic washable markers and paper to draw on.

 # Treasure Hunt in the Sandbox Game

What's more fun than digging for treasure in the sandbox? This game allows you a great excuse to dig in the dirt alongside your baby.

 ### How to Play

Show your baby a toy, then put it in the sandbox. Pour a little sand over it, then take it out and show it to your baby, saying, "Here's your toy." Then bury the toy deeper in the sand, leaving part of it exposed, and encourage him to dig it out. As your baby understands the game, hide the toy completely under the sand. Finally, hide several toys in the sand and encourage him to find all of them.

 ### Where and When

Outside during daylight hours is the best time to play this game.

 ### What You Are Teaching

Your baby is learning object permanence in this game.

 ### What You Need

Materials you need include a sandbox or tub filled with sand and toys or objects suitable to bury in the sand.

 ### Brainy Baby

On a rainy day—or if you don't have access to a sandbox or tub of sand—you can play "Treasure Hunt in the Sandbox" in another location. Fill a bowl or tub with water and bath bubbles, then hide toys beneath the bubbles. Put the bowl or tub in the bathtub if you don't want to mop floors after your baby is through playing.

The Least You Need to Know

- Babies learn object permanence around eight months, and games to develop this skill should be started around six months.

- Using photos, pictures, routines, and repetition help your baby develop good long-term memory and recall skills.

- Adding new elements to old favorite songs and stories challenges your baby to compare the new version with the old one; this is a great cognitive workout.

- Babies are able to recognize faces and objects around them before they are one year of age.

- Telling stories from your day helps your baby learn how to recall events and retell them in chronological order.

8

Introducing Problem-Solving Skills

In This Chapter

- ◆ Teaching your baby basic problem-solving skills, such as cause and effect
- ◆ Modeling problem-solving behavior for your baby
- ◆ Demonstrating size and number comparisons, such as "more than" and "bigger than"

Your baby will learn reasoning, logic, cause-and-effect, and other important problem-solving skills through exploration, trial-and-error, imitation, and role-playing. As you'll see, we encourage these activities throughout the chapter. In this chapter, we show you simple games you and your baby can play to interact with the world around you in a problem-solving way.

 What Should We Do About That Game

Babies don't automatically understand cause-and-effect or how to solve a problem. One of the best things you can do for your baby is to model problem-solving behaviors so he can start to learn them.

 ## How to Play

Throughout the day, model problem-solving behavior for your baby. For example, if you're out of peas for lunch, ask your baby, "What should we do about that? Let's have carrots instead." As your baby gets older, you can show a more sophisticated process: "We could go to the grocery store, but that would take a long time and we're hungry now. Let's put it on the list, though, so we don't forget next time. But what should we do about lunch? Should we have carrots instead?"

When your baby encounters a challenge on his own, do the same thing. For example, if his ball rolls under the table, ask "What should we do about that?" and then show or describe solutions to the problem.

 ## Where and When

This game can be played at any time, practically anywhere. You can also encourage others in the family to play this game with your baby—it can be a fun way for other children to interact with their younger sibling.

 ## What You Are Teaching

By modeling how you solve problems, you show your baby basic problem-solving skills.

 ## What You Need

Awareness of what you're doing and why during daily circumstances, so that you can communicate the process to your baby.

Baby Beware

Parents have a tendency to jump in and help their babies when their babies aren't sure how to do something. For example, if the ball rolls out of reach, you automatically get it and place it in your baby's hand. But the best thing you can do is give him a chance to figure out how to solve the problem. A ball just out of reach might encourage your baby to roll, crawl, or walk to get it—but he won't have the chance to learn if you solve all of his problems for him.

12+ months Big, Bigger, Biggest Game

Though your baby won't actually be sorting by size, color, or shape until she's 24 months or so, you can introduce the concept of sorting at an earlier age to get her started.

How to Play

Collect a small group of objects of similar appearance but different sizes. They could be bowls, boxes, pots, even stones from the backyard. Show them to your baby and place them in order of size. "This is a small rock. This one is a big rock. This one is even bigger. This is the biggest rock." Let your baby explore the objects, even if she doesn't sort them by size. (Be careful not to let her have small objects that she might swallow—babies learn about objects by stuffing them in their mouths!)

Where and When

Throughout the day, when your baby is alert and you have a few minutes to engage her, collect a few likely items and play this game. You can play it outdoors and indoors.

What You Are Teaching

You'll help your baby understand size comparison concepts by giving her the language she needs and showing her how the words relate to different objects.

What You Need

Use toys or objects that are somehow similar—such as blocks or books—but of varying sizes.

 More Than, Less Than Game

Introducing your baby to the concepts of "more than" and "less than" will help him develop his mathematical skills and spatial relationship skills.

How to Play

Show your baby the first group of objects, such as three toy cars. Count the cars and say, "There are three cars." Then show him the next group, such as five blocks. Count the blocks and say, "There are five blocks." Encourage him to count, too, by having him touch the objects while you count. Then say, "There are more blocks than cars." Add other groups of objects to help him compare numbers.

Where and When

You can play this game anywhere that you can gather together items to count.

What You Are Teaching

This game will help you demonstrate counting and helps your baby begin to understand number comparison.

What You Need

Collect groups of small objects or toys varying in number, such as three toy cars and five blocks.

Find the Picture Game

With this game, your baby actively participates in reading a book. While a young baby may get bored and restless just listening to you read, encouraging her to interact with you and the book will help her pay attention longer.

How to Play

With your baby sitting next to you, begin reading a story in a picture book. When the story mentions an object on the page, such as a rabbit, ask your baby, "Where is the rabbit?" A young baby won't be able to point, but she'll be able to touch the page with her hand. Reinforce her attempts to show you the picture. If you ask her to show you the cow and she touches the pig, simply say, "No, that's the pig. Where's the cow?" You can move her hand or the book so that she touches the cow.

Where and When

This game is best played when your child is ready to sit and read a book (in other words, when she isn't squirming around or trying to chase the cat).

What You Are Teaching

This game shows your baby that pictures represent real objects. We call a picture of a cat a "cat," just as we call a real cat a "cat."

What You Need

Use storybooks appropriate to your child's age to play this game. You can ask the children's librarian at your public library for guidance if you're not sure.

9+ months Does It Fit Game

Babies learn by exploring the world. This game encourages him to test out the concept of "fit" while you give him the words he needs to articulate the concept.

How to Play

Collect toys and objects and place them next to a box on the floor. Pick up one of the toys and ask your baby, "Does it fit?" Then try to put the toy in the box. Tell him if it fits or not. Then hand him one of the toys and encourage him to try to put it in the box. Ask, "Does it fit?" Allow him a moment to answer, but then say whether it fits or not. Do this for objects and toys that both do and don't fit in the box.

Where and When

This is a fun game to play when you have a few minutes at home.

What You Are Teaching

This game helps your baby begin to understand differences in sizes.

What You Need

You'll need a small box or container of some kind, and a group of toys to try and fit into the box. Some of the toys should be bigger than the box so they won't fit, while others should be small enough to easily fit.

 ### Brainy Baby

With any of the games in this chapter, let your baby choose whether he wants to play or not. If he doesn't seem interested or turns away from the game, stop and try later. Letting him make his own choices encourages great problem-solving skills.

9-12+ months What's Inside Game

Babies love figuring out how to open and close boxes, and they enjoy putting things in and taking them out. This game encourages your baby to think about what she's seeing and to correctly anticipate that what she puts in the box stays in the box until she, or you, take it out again.

 ### How to Play

Sit with your baby and put a toy inside a box. Close the lid. Ask your baby, "What's inside the box?" Then open the box and take the toy out. Say the name of the toy. Put that toy aside and place another one in the box. Ask, "What's inside the box now?" Open the box, take out the toy, and say its name. Next, encourage your baby to put a toy in the box, close the lid, then open it and take the toy out again.

 ### Where and When

Though this game is readily played at home, you can also play it in other places, especially when you need to distract your baby. For example, while waiting at the pediatrician's office, you can put an object in your purse or your pocket and play the game.

What You Are Teaching

This game helps your baby figure out the solution to a problem.

What You Need

All you need to play this game are a box and a few toys that fit into the box. Or you can improvise and put objects in your purse or your pocket. Be careful not to use objects that could pose a hazard to your baby.

6-9+ months Did Baby Do That Game

One of the problem-solving concepts your baby will learn is cause-and-effect—if he does something, something else happens as a consequence. For example, if he turns over his cup of milk, the milk falls onto the floor. This game helps him channel his curiosity in less messy ways.

 ### How to Play

Show your baby how to manipulate a toy to produce the desired result, for example, a jack-in-the-box or a squeaky toy. Then help him play with the toy by moving his hands to get the desired outcome, such as turning the handle to make the jack pop up or squeezing a toy to make it squeak.

An extremely low-tech version of this game is to make a sound when your baby touches your nose. He'll "beep" your nose over and over because it's so much fun to cause something to happen.

 ### Where and When

You can play this game anywhere with a toy that produces an effect when manipulated. Beware, though: the sound effects of some of these toys can be annoying, so you may not, for example, want to drive the other patrons of a restaurant nuts by playing the game there. The low-tech version, on the other hand, can be played anywhere.

 ### What You Are Teaching

This game shows your baby that when he does something, he can cause something else to happen.

 ### What You Need

For this game, pick activity toys, such as pop-up toys; squeaky toys; or a keyboard that require your baby to press buttons, turn handles, or move switches in order to produce specific results (particularly sounds) that can be repeated over and over.

Brainy Baby

Don't be discouraged if your baby figures out how to do something one day and forgets the next. It takes a while for your baby to master a skill so that he can do it regularly and routinely. And don't be surprised when your baby gets frustrated—there's so much to learn! Encourage his efforts, celebrate his successes, and don't worry about his failures.

10+ Which One Is It Game
months

This simple game can be done almost anywhere with almost anything. It can be a good game to distract your baby if you're waiting in line somewhere. It can also be used to teach your baby about the world around you.

How to Play

Sit with your baby on the floor or at the table (with your baby in a high chair). Put three small objects or toys in front of your baby (for example, a spoon, a cup, and a ball). Show her the spoon and say, "Spoon." Put it down and pick up the cup and say, "Cup." Do the same for the ball. Ask your baby to pick up the spoon. Then ask her to pick up the cup, and finally, the ball. If she doesn't understand the game at first, repeat it a few times.

Once she understands the game, you can play it with objects around you. For example, if you're in line at the post office, you can say, "Do you see the red shirt?" and encourage her to identify the person wearing the red shirt.

Where and When

Play this game anywhere by attending to what's happening around you and encouraging your baby to pay attention, too.

What You Are Teaching

This game helps your baby begin to recognize familiar objects and to match names to objects.

What You Need

To introduce the game, pick three small toys or other objects with simple names. Once your baby understands how the game is played, you can progress to using any object in the environment.

9+ months Guess Which Hand Game

Once your baby understands the concept of object permanence (see Chapter 7), you can play this game, which challenges him to develop reasoning skills.

 How to Play

Show your baby a small object or toy. Close your hand so the toy is hidden. Ask, "Where is the toy?" When your baby reaches for your hand, open it and say, "Yes, that's where the toy is." If he doesn't reach for the toy, open your hand and show it to him, saying, "Here's the toy." Then close your hand and ask again. He will soon learn to touch or gesture toward your hand.

When he's able to do that, close your hand around the toy and then close your other hand. Show both hands to your baby and ask, "Where is the toy?" Because he saw where you put it, he should be able to point to the hand that holds it. If he points to the wrong hand, open that hand and say, "No, not there. Where is it?" He will reason that it must be in your other hand and point to that. Eventually you can play the game without showing him where you put the object, and he will guess which hand.

 Where and When

This game doesn't require much in the way of materials or preparation, so you can play it practically anytime, anywhere.

 What You Are Teaching

Your baby will learn how to analyze a problem and develop problem-solving skills.

 What You Need

All you need for this game is a small object or toy that fits inside your hand. Remember to be careful of objects or toys that are small enough to pose a choking hazard to your baby.

 Which Lid Fits Game

Most babies enjoy playing with pots and pans, because they see you using them to make meals. This game does more than entertain your baby, though—it encourages her to figure out how the pieces fit together.

How to Play

Start by showing your baby one pot with a lid that fits it. Show her how the lid goes on the pot. Once she understands how it works, give her a different-sized lid. Encourage her to work out whether that lid fits, too. Ask, "Does that fit? It's too big, isn't it?" Add more pots and lids as she figures out the concept.

Where and When

You can play this game at home in the kitchen, anytime—it's an especially good distraction to use during meal preparation.

What You Are Teaching

This game helps your baby develop problem-solving skills. It also introduces comparison skills and the language needed to describe the concepts: "bigger than" and "smaller than."

What You Need

For this game, you'll use pots of varying sizes with matching lids. You can also use toy dishes.

Brainy Baby

You can encourage your baby's learning by sitting where she can clearly see your face while playing, and by allowing her time to respond to prompts and questions (even if she doesn't). Also, modeling behaviors, acknowledging her efforts, and becoming involved in your baby's play is important in order for her to learn.

 # What If Game

Babies learn problem-solving skills by using their imaginations. This game helps your baby develop his reasoning skills.

How to Play

Show your baby a picture of a duck. Ask, "What sound does a duck make?" He may try to quack, or you may have to quack to show him. Then ask, "What if Lawrence was a duck? What would he sound like?" Ask, "What if Mommy was a duck? What would she sound like?" You can also add movements, such as flapping your arms like wings.

Where and When

This is a good game to play when your baby is ready to sit still for a while but isn't too sleepy to participate. You can do it anywhere you can read a book to him.

What You Are Teaching

This game teaches your baby some basic logic skills.

What You Need

You'll find this game is easiest to play with storybooks that have simple pictures of farm animals.

Wrap the Toy Game

Babies like good surprises. This game turns old toys into something new while encouraging your baby to figure out how to unwrap the toy.

How to Play

Wrap a couple of small toys in wrapping paper, or the comics from the newspaper. Make them easy to open—not a lot of tape or ribbons. Tear a corner of the paper to show your baby that something's inside. Watch her figure out how to get to the toy, and watch her surprise at seeing a "new" toy emerge—even if it is an old favorite.

Where and When

You don't need to wait for your baby's birthday to introduce her to the joys of unwrapping presents. You can play this game at home anytime you have a few minutes to wrap and unwrap toys—the "wrapping" can be as simple as a towel wrapped around a toy.

What You Are Teaching

You wouldn't think that opening presents would build cognitive skills, but it does! This game helps your baby develop her problem-solving abilities.

What You Need

All you need is a toy (or two) and something to wrap it in—that could be wrapping paper, newspaper, or a kitchen towel.

 What Do Animals Do All Day Game

Babies like to hear about the familiar—in this case, what happens during the course of a day—and they also love to hear about animals doing human activities. This game helps your baby build his reasoning skills.

How to Play

Pick an animal familiar to your baby and ask, "What does cow do all day?" Then talk about the cow going through the course of a day similar to your baby's typical day. For example, the cow wakes up, has breakfast, plays outside, comes in for lunch, and so on. Let your baby join in the story however he's able. Ask him questions such as "What's next for cow?"

Where and When

When your baby is older, this game can be played anywhere, but when he's younger, he's more likely to enjoy it at home, with toys that represent the animals you're talking about.

What You Are Teaching

This game calls on your baby to use his reasoning skills to figure out what happens next, by comparing what the animal is doing to what he does in a typical day. The game also encourages imagination and role-playing skills.

What You Need

Your baby will understand this game if you introduce it using concrete objects, such as a collection of wooden or plastic baby-safe animals. You can also use boxes or containers that represent beds, barns, feeding troughs—whatever the animals need to do their daily activities.

10+ months Upside Down or Right Side Up Game

Your baby knows how things *should* look. This game challenges her to decide if something is in its correct position and, if not, to do something about it.

How to Play

Take a cup and put it upside down on the floor. Ask your baby, "Is the cup upside down or right side up?" Then say, "It's upside down! Lets fix it." Turn the cup right side up. Say, "That's better." For children over 12 months, ask questions to help your baby decide: "Can Petra put milk in the cup? No. That means the cup is upside down."

Where and When

This game is fun to play when your baby is alert and active and ready to explore. It can be played almost anywhere.

What You Are Teaching

By playing this game, you'll teach your baby how to solve problems, and you'll introduce *prepositional concepts*.

BABY BABBLE

Prepositional concepts show how objects are related to each other and the world around them. For example, "in," "under," and "on." Your baby will master these concepts through exploration of the world around her, and it helps if you give her the words she needs to describe the concepts.

What You Need

For your baby to understand this game, you'll want to use objects that have a definitive front and back or top and bottom, such as a stuffed animal or a cup.

 9+ **You Choose Game**
months

One of the ways that babies learn problem-solving skills is by imitating others. This game also encourages turn-taking and thinking about and communicating what your baby wants.

 How to Play

Set out three or four toys to play with, then say to your baby, "Mama wants to play with the ball." Pick up the ball and play with it (and your baby) for just a few seconds. Then put it down and say, "What does Clarence want to play with?" Encourage your baby to pick one of the toys. When he does, play with the toy with him.

You can do the same at snacktime. Show your baby two snacks and say, "Mama wants animal crackers." Take some out of the box and put them on your plate. Ask, "What snack does Clarence want?" At first he will probably choose whatever you choose, but over time he will begin to communicate his own preferences.

 Where and When

You can incorporate this game throughout the day as you do various activities with your baby.

 What You Are Teaching

This game helps your baby begin to develop decision-making and problem-solving skills. As your baby gets older, you can start to describe your reasons for choosing as you do, and that will further model decision-making skills.

 What You Need

You can use your baby's regular toys or snacks to play this game.

What Floats, What Doesn't Game

Babies love water games, and this one helps them use their observational skills to reach conclusions.

 ### How to Play

Fill a container about half full with water and put it in the bathtub or on a towel outside. Put water-safe objects or toys next to your baby. Show her how to put them in the container (or in the bathtub if she is actually taking a bath). As your baby puts the objects in the container, say, "Look, that object floats!" or "That objects sinks!" Describe the objects: "That comb is made of plastic. See how it floats on top of the water," or "That truck is made of metal. See how it sinks to the bottom."

 ### Where and When

You can play this game in the bathtub during your baby's regular bathtime. It's also a fun game to play outside on a nice day, during playtime.

 ### What You Are Teaching

You'll help your baby learn reasoning and problem-solving skills as she observes how the objects act.

What You Need

Pick small water-safe toys—or objects of various sizes and weights—to play this game. Be sure to pick some that will float and others that won't. You'll also need a clear container or tub so that your baby can see the objects. And don't forget the towels!

The Least You Need to Know

- Through observation, exploration, and imitation, your baby begins to master basic problem-solving skills.

- Model the skills you want your baby to develop.

- Your baby needs plenty of opportunities to figure out how to solve problems herself, without you jumping in and assisting her.

- Describing why you make the choices you make and solve your problems the way you do helps your baby gain a better understanding of how he can make choices and solve problems, too.

Chapter 9

Teaching Your Baby About His/Her World

In This Chapter

- ◆ Showing your baby ways to interact with the world

- ◆ Familiarizing your baby with what his world looks like

- ◆ Encouraging your baby to use all of her senses to explore her surroundings

- ◆ Helping your baby learn about the world by acting as an intermediary when he can't do it himself

By encouraging active exploration, you not only help her understand the world she's in, but you help her develop all of her senses. In this chapter, we show you games you can play to help your baby become more familiar with her surroundings and the things in it.

6-9+ months **Describe the Food Game**

Giving your baby the words to describe what he's feeling, seeing, and tasting helps him organize and understand the world around him.

How to Play

When you're feeding your baby, describe what you're feeding him, how it tastes, how it feels, and what it looks like. Take a bite of his food and tell him what you think.

Where and When

You can play this game anywhere at mealtime or snacktime.

What You Are Teaching

Your baby learns the words associated with the environment around him.

What You Need

Use foods with different textures, colors, and tastes to play this game.

Brainy Baby

When describing food to your baby, use specific words such as "soft," and "salty." Other descriptive words might be smooth, crunchy, sour, firm, slimy, sweet, sharp, bitter, chewy, greasy, and mushy.

9+ months **Hide and Seek Game**

In this version of hide and seek, the toys are hiding and the baby is seeking.

How to Play

When your baby starts crawling, put a few of her favorite toys in various locations around the house. For example, you might put a stuffed animal under a table or lean a doll against a wall. Your baby will be encouraged to explore her surroundings by finding her favorite toys in unexpected places.

Where and When

You can play this game at home anytime that your baby is feeling active and wants to crawl around and explore.

What You Are Teaching

This game teaches your baby about exploration and its rewards— you never know what you might discover!

What You Need

All you need to play this game are a few of your baby's favorite toys, strategically located around the house.

 What's This for Game

This game goes beyond simply labeling the objects that your baby encounters every day. It encourages him to think about and explore how those objects are used.

How to Play

Show your baby an object he uses every day and ask him, "What's this for?" Then use the object for that purpose. For example, pick up his hairbrush and ask, "What's this for?" Give him a moment to respond, then say, "The brush is used to brush Parker's hair." Then brush your baby's hair.

Where and When

You can play this game throughout the day as you go about your daily activities with your baby.

What You Are Teaching

Playing this game shows your baby the functions of everyday objects.

What You Need

To play this game, you can use everyday objects that you ordinarily use with your baby, such as a baby-safe brush or comb.

 What Is Mommy Doing Game

Your baby is intensely curious about what you do and why you do it, even when it seems obvious to you.

How to Play

As you go about your daily activities, encourage your baby to interact with you about what you're doing. Instead of just describing your actions, ask, "What is Mommy doing?" Give her a chance to answer, then tell her, "Mommy is fixing breakfast."

Where and When

You can easily play this game anytime, anywhere, throughout the day. Just remember to interact with your baby even if what you're doing seems boring and mundane!

What You Are Teaching

This game helps your baby become familiar with ordinary routines and daily activities.

What You Need

All this game requires is for you to be aware of and talk about your daily activities and routines.

6+ months What Is Baby Doing Game

As with the "What is Mommy Doing Game," this game encourages your baby to interact with you and explore what he is doing and why.

How to Play

As your baby does his normal activities, don't just describe them; ask him about them. "What is Tony doing now? Tony, did you just put that toy in your mouth?" Use time markers when you ask, such as "What will Tony do next?"

Where and When

This game can also be played anywhere throughout the day. You can include other "players" in this game when they're available, and have them ask questions, too.

What You Are Teaching

This game helps build your baby's familiarity with routines and daily activities.

What You Need

You don't need anything special to play this game—you just need to interact with your baby throughout the day.

9+ months What's in the House Game

Your older baby loves to explore, but she's not quite able to do everything she'd like to do. With your help, she can learn more about her environment.

How to Play

Take your baby around the house and explore it. Show her things she can't see from her level. Let her touch a painting or a silk flower. Describe what she's seeing. Let her interact with her surroundings (for example, pulling a book from a bookshelf), as long as it isn't dangerous.

Where and When

This is an exciting game to play at home—as well as other familiar places—especially when your baby is feeling alert and active and you want to direct her energies.

What You Are Teaching

This game allows your baby to learn about her surroundings by encouraging her to explore them.

What You Need

You don't need anything special to play this game—just your home and other familiar places.

9+ months What's Outside Game

The world outside can stimulate all of your baby's senses—sight, sound, touch, taste, and smell. Give him the opportunity to explore parts of the outside world he couldn't without your help.

How to Play

Bring your baby outside and encourage him to use all of his senses to learn about the outdoors. (Carefully supervise, though, so he doesn't taste or touch something dangerous.) Have him touch the bark of a tree, listen to a bird, or splash in a puddle. You can also bring him outside after the sun has set to show him the moon and the stars.

Where and When

Play this game anytime you're outside. It doesn't matter where—in the backyard or at the corner park work.

What You Are Teaching

Your baby will learn to explore by playing this game with you.

What You Need

All you need to play this game are the natural surroundings in your front- or backyard or in a park.

Brainy Baby

If you have other children, engage in a scavenger hunt so that the "What's Outside Game" can include everyone. Before you go, make a list of items—a fallen leaf, a white stone—then collect all of the items on the list.

6+ months This Is the Way to Grandma's House Game

Babies love songs, and this one encourages her to think about and observe her surroundings.

How to Play

To the tune of "To Grandmother's House We Go" (or any song with a rhythm you can easily remember), describe in a song how you get to the special places that you and your baby like to visit. Describe landmarks you drive past, stoplights you stop at, and houses and buildings you see along the way.

Where and When

The best place to play this game is in the car while driving to your favorite places.

What You Are Teaching

You'll encourage your baby to observe her surroundings by playing this game during car trips. While it's most fun to play the game while you're on the way to grandma's house, you can also play it on the way to the grocery store or the gas station.

What You Need

This game simply requires regular trips to special or favorite places.

6+ months Teaching Your Baby About People Around Him Game

This game uses the photo album you created in Chapter 7 for "Favorite People Game." You'll use your loved ones' photo album to do more than show your baby photos of the people in his life.

How to Play

In Chapter 7, we showed how you could name the people in the photo album, remind your baby of his loved ones before they come to visit, and tell stories about his loved ones. In this game, you use the photo album to help your baby recognize his similarities to and differences from those people. For example, point to a sibling and say, "Greg has red hair just like you do!" You could describe a loved one's likes and dislikes and give physical characteristics, comparing them to your baby.

Where and When

This is a wonderful quiet time game to play with your baby at home, when he is willing to sit for a few minutes and look at pictures.

What You Are Teaching

This games helps your baby learn to recognize loved ones, and helps him learn and remember the characteristics of the people in your baby's life.

What You Need

You'll need a photo album of loved ones to play this game.

6-9+ months What Happens Next Game

Babies love cause-and-effect games. This one teaches your baby about her environment and encourages her to explore.

How to Play

With your baby in your arms, turn off the light switch. Say, "Off!" Then turn on the switch and say, "On!" Then help her manipulate the switch. Say, "Mindy flipped the switch. What happened? The light turned on." You can go through the house finding light switches to turn on and off. You can also demonstrate other simple mechanisms around the house (such as the doorbell and water faucet).

Where and When

You can play this game anywhere there are light switches, though it's probably best not to play it in places where people will complain about the lights going on and off.

What You Are Teaching

While it may seem your baby is only manipulating a switch and maybe laughing when the lights go on and off, this game is actually teaching your baby about cause-and-effect and the importance of exploring her environment.

What You Need

This game requires working light switches—and a place where people don't mind the lights going off and on.

 Baby Beware

Be sure to carefully supervise your baby and baby-proof your home. As your baby becomes more active and explores, she becomes a bigger danger to herself than when she was small and inactive. See Chapter 3 for more information on baby-proofing your home.

6+ months Singing to Activities Game

You don't have to be a rhyming genius to engage your baby's interest and attention. Simply singing about what you're doing instead of just telling about it gets his attention.

 How to Play

Sing along to your activities as you do them. Your baby will find the singing interesting and will learn about the activities as you sing about them. Sing "This is the way we wash our clothes" and then describe "lights in this pile, colors in that; open the lid and put them in," and so on.

Where and When

This is another fun game to play at home while doing routine chores and activities.

What You Are Teaching

You'll teach your baby familiarity with daily activities and chores—and you may make them a little more fun for yourself.

 What You Need

The courage to sing!

 Gathering Treasures Game

Collecting treasures is a fun pastime that serves as a visual reminder of your baby's history.

 How to Play

When your baby expresses interest in a certain toy or object, you can encourage her to "collect" the toy or object and put it in a treasure box. If you're on a field trip, you may want to collect treasures that will help you remember the trip, such as shells and stones. If you plan to let her have unsupervised access to her treasure box, make sure the objects are safe for her to play with, chew on, and otherwise explore.

Where and When

You can play this game at home anytime, but it can be most fun and most meaningful if you play it while you're on a trip to a special place.

What You Are Teaching

Your baby will learn observation skills, plus she'll gain an appreciation of the environment through directly experiencing it.

What You Need

A treasure box (see Chapter 13, "Create a Treasure Box Game" for how to make one).

Brainy Baby

If there are some items in your baby's treasure box that she shouldn't touch unsupervised, put the box on a closet shelf and take it down occasionally to look through together, talking about the treasures and where you and your baby found them.

 # Draw in the Snow, Mud, or Sand Game

Put on some old clothes and don't be afraid to get messy! With this game, you'll encourage your baby to explore the outdoors and leave his mark on the world (at least until the snow melts, the mud dries, or the tide comes in).

 ## How to Play

When it snows, bundle up and bring your baby outside, not for a snowball fight but for a drawing game. Show him how to draw in the snow. Draw simple pictures with a stick or other tool and encourage your baby to do the same. He may want to leave footprints or snow angels, and that's fine, too. For those in climates without snow, you can play in the mud or the sand just the same way.

 ## Where and When

This game is a good excuse to get outside and play—weather permitting, of course.

 ## What You Are Teaching

By playing this game, you'll teach your baby the pleasures of interacting with nature.

 ## What You Need

All you need to play this game are sticks or other objects to draw and make marks with—and some snow (or mud or sand) to draw in.

 # How the Bathroom Works Game

Though your baby won't be interested in toilet training until she's a bit older, you can spend some time exploring the bathroom so that she's familiar with it when it does come time to shed the diapers for good.

How to Play

Take your baby around the bathroom and show her how every-thing works. Brush your hair and your teeth. Let your baby manipulate the brushes. Show her how the faucet works and flush the toilet. This makes the bathroom a friendlier environment for her.

Where and When

This game is a fun one to play at home in your bathroom, at any time. Because there's so much to do in the bathroom, it can be a nice distraction from behaviors and activities you don't want your baby engaging in.

What You Are Teaching

You'll help your baby learn to explore the environment around her by playing this game.

What You Need

You just need a bathroom to play this game—though considering how babies play, you'll want to make sure it's clean (and safe).

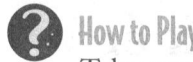 See Baby's World Game

We see the world at our level and don't always appreciate what our babies are seeing. This game helps grown-ups see what the world looks like from their baby's point of view.

How to Play

Pretend you are your baby's size. Get down on your belly next to your baby and look around. Tell him what you see and what the world is like from the floor. Describe what you smell, hear, and feel like being down at his level.

Where and When

You can play this game anytime you're at home and willing to get on the floor and look around.

What You Are Teaching

This game teaches your baby not just about exploring the environment, but sharing it, too.

 ### What You Need

You need an environment to explore and a reasonably comfortable spot on the floor to explore it from.

 ## 6+ months Show Baby's World Through Photos Game

Babies love seeing pictures of familiar places almost as much as they love seeing pictures of familiar faces.

 ### How to Play

Take photos of your baby's room and places around the house and outside where she frequently goes. Put them in a photo album. Show her the pictures, naming the rooms and the objects in them. You can do the same for other favorite places. Then, when she's going to visit her grandmother's house, you can show her the rooms in the photo album and remind her of what it's like there.

 ### Where and When

You can play this game at home, anytime your baby is willing to sit and look at pictures with you. It's especially fun to play just before you go to visit a special place, to remind your baby of where you're going and what it's like there.

 ### What You Are Teaching

This game teaches your baby familiarity with her environment.

 ### What You Need

For this game, you'll need to be able to take pictures, so you'll want a camera, either digital or the old-fashioned kind. You'll also need a way to produce the photos, whether that's printing them out on your computer or bringing a roll of film to a photo lab. Then you'll need a photo album to put the photos in.

The Least You Need to Know

- Utilizing active exploration will help your baby learn about her surroundings.

- Encouraging your baby to use all of his senses will help him to make sense of his world.

- Interacting with her environment gives your baby confidence and helps her understand the world around her.

- Singing about what you're doing attracts your baby's attention and gets him interested in your activities.

Stimulating Your Baby's Social and Emotional Development

In this part, we'll show you games and activities you can use to help your baby relax and learn to calm himself down and become more independent and self-reliant. We'll also give you lots of things to do to encourage your baby to imitate and pretend.

10

Calming Your Baby

In This Chapter

- ◆ Simple techniques to help your baby relax
- ◆ Self-calming activities your baby can use to soothe himself
- ◆ How to keep yourself calm so you can deal with your upset baby
- ◆ Effective bedtime transition techniques
- ◆ The importance of activities that develop trust and reassurance

Sometimes you need activities to help your baby wind down at bedtime so that putting your baby to bed doesn't become a battle of wills. Even better, you'd like to know how to get him started in learning how to self-calm, so that he'll eventually be able to calm himself down without your intervention. In this chapter, we'll show you games and activities you can do with your baby to help him calm down when he's upset, tired, or overstimulated.

Take a Big Breath In Game

Once a baby is upset, she sometimes doesn't know how to turn off the waterworks even after the reason she became upset is resolved. This game can help her get a grip on her emotions (you, too!). As she gets older, your baby will be able to use the technique to soothe herself.

 ### How to Play

With your baby in your lap or while you're holding her, say, "Wow, Nikky is really upset! Take a deep breath, Nikki." Then show her how to take a deep breath in, inhaling through your nose until your chest expands, then exhaling through your mouth.

Say, "Can you do that, Nikki?" and encourage her to imitate you. The deep breaths will help her calm down, though she may not get the hang of it until after a few repetitions.

 ### Where and When

This is a simple technique you can use anywhere and anytime your baby is upset. You may find it helps to take a deep breath in yourself!

 ### What You Are Teaching

You can introduce your baby to self-soothing skills with this activity—something that she'll use rest of her life whenever she's stressed.

 ### What You Need

Patience, as it may take a little time for your baby to calm down enough to pay attention to you and start taking deep breaths.

Goodnight, Stuffed Bear Game

Creating calming bedtime rituals helps your baby transition to sleep time and reduces the numbers of upsets when it's time to go to bed.

How to Play

At bedtime, once your baby is ready to be put in his crib, bring him around the house and quietly say goodnight to his family and his favorite toys. Keep it very low-key. Say, "It's bedtime for Charlie. Goodnight, Daddy." Then let Daddy give a hug or a kiss, again keeping things quiet and low-key. Say goodnight to his favorite toys: "Goodnight, truck. Goodnight, stuffed bear." Then put your baby to bed.

Where and When

This activity is part of a daily routine you can do at home, at bedtime. Some parts of the ritual could be used to help soothe your baby at bedtime even if you're not at home, although you may not be able to reproduce every aspect of the routine.

What You Are Teaching

This ritual shows your baby the soothing nature of routines and rituals and helps your baby learn to anticipate what happens next.

What You Need

This goodnight ritual needs consistency to succeed, so be sure to set aside time every night to do it.

 Wrapping Baby in a Blanket

Younger babies can often be soothed by wrapping them in a blanket—often called swaddling. This helps your baby feel warm and secure.

What to Do

You may have been shown how to swaddle your baby at the hospital when she was born. If not, you can simply wrap your baby snuggly—but not too tightly—in a blanket, making sure her head is free and that she's breathing comfortably. Think burrito and you'll have the gist of it. You can use a sling-type carrier instead to get a similar effect. Talk to your baby in a comforting way the whole time you are wrapping her up, so she can be soothed by your voice as well.

Don't wrap your baby if the room is very warm—not only will that make her uncomfortable, but overheating is a risk factor for SIDS (Sudden Infant Death Syndrome).

Where and When
When your baby is very young, you can use this technique anytime she is upset. As she gets a little older, you can use it before bedtime to help calm her down.

What You Are Teaching
The security of being wrapped in a blanket helps reassure your baby and build her trust in you.

What You Need
This technique requires a small, comfortable blanket to fit around your baby.

3+ months Keeping It Quiet

Here is another activity that helps your baby transition smoothly to bedtime with a minimum of fuss and upset.

What to Do
Thirty minutes to an hour before bedtime, announce that it's quiet time. With your baby, go through the house and turn off unnecessary lights, put away toys, and otherwise signal that it's getting to be bedtime. Use your quiet time voice as you interact with your baby, and pick calm activities, like a warm bath and reading aloud, before you put your baby to bed.

Where and When
This routine can be done at home at bedtime. The more consistent you are, the more successful it will be in helping your baby transition to nighttime.

What You Are Teaching
This activity shows your baby that the soothing nature of routines and rituals can be comforting and relaxing. It also helps her learn to anticipate what happens next.

What You Need

This ritual will make the most sense to your baby if you do it at home consistently.

 # Birth + Avoiding Overstimulation

Babies can become fussy when they're overstimulated and too much is going on around them. Every baby has a different threshold for overstimulation, and it can vary depending on other factors as well—if your baby is tired or teething, for example, he may be more easily stressed by his environment than he is normally.

 ### What to Do

If your baby is upset, and it's not because of something obvious, like being hungry or wet, he may be overstimulated. This is especially common if he's visiting family or involved in a special event—something that doesn't happen every day. Even loving attention can be too much for a baby, so take him away from all of that. Leave the room, go outside, find a quiet place, and just let your baby be for a little while.

 ### Where and When

Use this technique anywhere, anytime your baby is upset and you suspect that he is overstimulated (rather than something you can easily fix, such being hungry).

 ### What You Are Teaching

By responding to your baby's cues, you're reassuring your baby that you're there to comfort him. You also build his trust in you.

 ### What You Need

To avoid overstimulation of your baby, you need to be aware of the circumstances and conditions under which it's likely your baby will be overstimulated. Pay attention and act on what you know. You know your baby best, so don't be afraid to say no to—or limit the amount of time you spend at—events that you know will overstimulate him.

12+ months Tighten then Loosen Game

This game is based on progressive muscle relaxation, a technique that adults and older children can use to help relax. Though your baby won't be able to do it by herself for a while, you'll be giving her the foundation for a skill she can use all of her life.

? How to Play

Show your child how to tighten her muscles by making a fist. Say "Tight!" and make a fist, encouraging your child to do the same. Then say "Loose!" and relax your hand, shaking your arm loosely. You may also encourage her to push her foot against your hand to tighten her leg muscles, or you may scrunch your shoulders and encourage her to do the same to tighten that muscle group. Remember to use "tight" and "loose" as cues.

Where and When

You can play this game anytime and anywhere, but it's especially effective if you sense that your baby is tense or stressed.

What You Are Teaching

This game teaches your baby how to use relaxation techniques. It also shows her how physical activity can help reduce stressful feelings.

What You Need

You don't need anything special to play this game—just your body and a little patience to teach the technique.

Birth + Swinging the Baby Game

This game simulates the rocking motion that your baby felt when he was still in your womb. It can help soothe him. However, if he's really upset and thrashing around, try another activity first, because he'll need to stay still for this game.

 ### How to Play

This game requires two adults. Lay your baby on his back on a blanket. Have an adult hold each end of the blanket. Carefully lift the blanket with your baby in it. Swing him slowly and gently in the blanket. Smile at him and sing a soothing song while swinging him.

 ### Where and When

You can play this game at home whenever your baby is fussy or upset. Your baby will need to be able to stay still to play the game, so make sure he's not too upset before you start.

 ### What You Are Teaching

This game helps soothe your baby through the rocking motion. It also helps build trust and reassurance. Even more, it requires your baby to concentrate on his physical balance, so it's a game that helps develop motor skills, too.

 ### What You Need

You'll need a blanket and another adult to play this game.

 # Touching the Baby Game

An upset baby can easily turn your stomach into knots. This activity can help both of you calm down and relax.

 ### How to Play

Hold your baby and touch her face, gently stroking her cheek. Tell her how much you love her. Say her name. Remember to keep your own voice calm and loving. If your baby is older and kicking and squirming from being upset, then put her in her crib and stroke her back or her tummy, again telling her how much you love her while saying her name.

 ### Where and When

This game is so low-tech you can do it anywhere, anytime. You don't have to wait until your baby is upset, either. Your baby will enjoy this game whenever you want to play it.

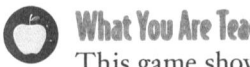

What You Are Teaching

This game shows your baby the soothing and healing nature of being touched by loved ones.

What You Need

It's best if you're not stressed yourself when you play this game, because your stressed feelings can be transferred in your touch. So you'll need the ability to be calm and relaxed when your baby is not.

Birth + Doing Something New Game

Upset babies often abandon being upset when they get distracted by something new. This game capitalizes on that tendency.

How to Play

When your usual tricks aren't working to soothe your baby, try introducing something new:

- ◆ If you usually walk your baby, rock him or take him for a drive.

- ◆ Bring out a new toy.

- ◆ If you have other children, ask one of them to calm him down.

- ◆ If you usually read to him at bedtime, try singing instead.

- ◆ Call a loved one on the phone and invite your baby to listen to that person's voice.

Where and When

You can use these techniques anytime your baby is upset, using whichever ones are appropriate to where you are and what time of day it is.

What You Are Teaching

Through paying attention to your baby's needs and by trying to distract him from his upset, you show him how to develop self-soothing skills. You also teach him to trust you and to be reassured by your actions.

What You Need

All you need are some ideas for things you can do to distract your baby when he's upset. Since it's hard to think of them when your baby is screaming in your ear, do some brainstorming ahead of time, thinking about things your baby likes to do that have calmed him down in the past.

 # Birth + Tummy Rocking Game

Babies love to feel a rocking motion. Instead of using a rocking chair, this game shows you how to rock your baby on her tummy, which means she also gets the opportunity to practice lifting her head.

Babies with colic may be soothed by the pressure on their tummy and the rocking motion of this game.

 ### How to Play

Put a bolster pillow (a cylinder-shaped pillow) or big ball on the floor. Place your baby tummy down on it. Make sure the bolster or ball supports her torso, neck, and thighs. Help her turn her head to one side. Gently rock her back and forth while singing a nursery rhyme or lullaby that she likes.

 ### Where and When

You can play this game at home—or anywhere there's a clean floor and a pillow—at any time.

 ### What You Are Teaching

This game helps your baby learn to expect soothing from caregivers (and therefore to trust them). It also requires her to use her motor skills to maintain physical balance.

 ### What You Need

You'll need a bolster pillow or a ball large enough to support and rock your baby on.

 Let's Find Daddy Game

As with the "Something New Game," this game uses the tendency of babies to be interested in something new to help soothe them.

How to Play

If you've tried your best to calm your baby down and your best isn't working, play this game. This could be any other caregiver your baby knows and loves. Hand over the baby to this person and disappear. Even if the second caregiver can't calm your baby down, a few minutes' respite may make all the difference in how you handle the stress of the situation.

Where and When

You can play this game whenever you've reached your limit and need to take a break from trying to soothe your baby, so long as you can find a trusted adult to hand your baby off to.

What You Are Teaching

By knowing when you're getting too stressed to deal effectively with your baby, you're teaching your baby to trust that you'll always do the right thing for him. By involving others in caring for your baby when he is upset, you'll teach him that many people love him—a very reassuring concept to learn.

What You Need

To play this game, you need another caregiver your baby knows and loves.

Show a Little Respect

Sometimes we can get frustrated and annoyed with a crying or upset baby when she can't communicate what's wrong. Just imagine how frustrated and annoyed your baby must be for the exact same reason. This activity helps everyone try to understand and communicate effectively in frustrating situations.

What to Do

When your baby is upset, acknowledge and validate her feelings—and yours, too! "Michelle is crying. Michelle must be sad about something. Mama wishes she knew why. Can Michelle say why she is sad?" Give your baby a chance to answer, though she may not be able to. Reinforcing that you recognize her feelings may help her calm down.

Where and When

You can do this activity play this game anywhere, anytime your baby is upset. You can also teach other people in the family to play, so that everyone learns to communicate their feelings.

What You Are Teaching

By reinforcing that emotions and needs are real—and that you have them, too—you'll reassure your baby and help build her trust in you. You'll also validate her and show that you respect her emotions.

What You Need

You'll need patience and the ability to respectfully articulate what you're feeling or don't understand.

Birth + Putting Yourself in Your Baby's Shoes

Your baby isn't a creature from another planet, or unknown and unknowable. This activity encourages you to use your imagination to figure out what your baby needs and how to soothe him.

What to Do

When your baby is upset and you're not sure how to comfort him, put yourself in his place. Would you want someone bouncing you on their knee if you were mad about something they did? Probably not. What would help you calm down? Maybe a quiet walk, or being left alone for a few minutes. Maybe a hug, or a gentle massage. Then try those ideas out and see if they help your baby calm down.

Where and When

You can try this technique whenever your baby is upset, no matter where it happens.

 ### What You Are Teaching

By trying to understand what your baby is feeling and what would make him feel better, you develop strategies and techniques that can help soothe him, building his trust in you and reassuring him that you will do all you can to comfort him.

 ### What You Need

For this technique to be effective, you need to have empathy for your baby—and a bit of an imagination so you can think about solutions to your baby's problem.

The Least You Need to Know

- Showing your baby relaxation techniques will eventually help her learn to soothe herself when she's upset.

- When you're baby is upset, it can be frustrating for everyone, so keeping yourself calm is crucial.

- Babies respond to tried-and-true techniques, but they may also respond to something new.

- By establishing rituals and routines at bedtime, you can help your baby calmly make this transition.

- Babies can be easily overstimulated, so seek out quiet times and places when your baby is upset.

Helping Your Baby Become More Self-Reliant

In This Chapter

- ◆ Encouraging self-reliance through persistence
- ◆ Developing necessary independence skills
- ◆ Creating opportunities for exploration
- ◆ Giving your baby a say in what he does, eats, and wears

All babies have a drive to discover how the world works and how they can manipulate objects in their environment. By encouraging that drive, you'll also encourage your baby's love of learning. In this chapter, we show you games and activities you can do to encourage independence in your baby.

I Can Do It Game

Babies love to imitate other people, and they also love the feeling that they can do the same things bigger people can. This game helps your baby develop skills she'll need to perform activities of daily living as she gets older.

 ## How to Play

Encourage your baby to do what you're doing. For example, let her push the stroller, or give her a cloth and ask her to help you wipe off the table. At first she won't be too coordinated, but she'll love doing what the big people do.

 ## Where and When

You can play this game at home anytime you're engaged in daily activities that your baby can take part in.

What You Are Teaching

By encouraging your baby to get involved in the activities of daily living, you teach her self-reliance skills. You'll also help her develop her motor skills, since everyday tasks such as wiping off a table require focus, coordination of muscles, and fine and gross motor skills.

 ## What You Need

Your child will be most successful if you provide child-size versions of adult tools, such as strollers and toolboxes. You can also provide her with "adult" tools that she can manipulate, like a cloth to wipe off the table.

 **Brainy Baby**

If you have other children, encourage them to play the "I Can Do It Game," too. Have them show your baby how to manipulate a broom, or have both children sweep at the same time. Ask your older child to show your baby how to take a stuffed animal for a walk in the stroller (if your baby is walking).

You Can Do It Game

By recognizing when your baby is showing signs of independence, and praising him when it happens, you'll encourage his growth.

How to Play

Whenever you see your baby try a new skill or reach a new milestone, as simple as turning over or taking his first steps, be sure to encourage him in his efforts. Say, "You did it!" and "You can do it!" to help your baby become more confident in his attempts to manipulate the world around him.

Where and When

Play this game anywhere, whenever your baby tries something new. Encourage other family members and loved ones to play it, too—what's new to them may be old hat to you, but it will still encourage your baby.

What You Are Teaching

By approving of and encouraging attempts at independence, you're teaching your baby to value self-reliance.

What You Need

All you'll need for this game is awareness of your baby's attempts to try new things.

Wash Baby's Face Game

You will wash your baby's face so many times, it's a great opportunity to make a game out of it! You can also play this as "Dry Baby Off Game" by using a towel after a bath, instead of a washcloth during a bath.

How to Play

Get a washcloth wet and wring it out. Touch it to your baby's chin, then say, "Wash Breanna's chin!" Give her the cloth and help her wash her chin. Then touch her nose and say, "Wash Breanna's nose!" again helping her do it. You can also expand the game to include other body parts, such as hands, elbows, and toes. The same goes for drying off; say, "Dry Breanna's tummy and toes!"

Where and When

Play this game during bathtime or clean-up time. You can do it at the sink or in the bathtub.

What You Are Teaching

By talking about your baby's body parts as you play this game, you'll help build your baby learn body awareness. By encouraging her to use the wash cloth or towel herself, you'll foster her independence skills and self-care skills.

What You Need

For this game, you just need a washcloth or a towel—and some water!

9-12+ months Pass the Jelly Game

This game, while messy, is a fun one for your baby to play. It encourages him to manipulate objects to get what he wants and fosters his independence and confidence.

How to Play

Dip a spoon in some jelly and spread it on the cracker. Offer a bite to your baby. Then give the spoon and a cracker to your baby, saying, "Ben try!" Let him dip the spoon in the jelly (give him guidance if needed) and spread it on his cracker.

Where and When

Because this is a messy game, it's best played at home. Do it at snacktime or mealtime—ideally not when your baby is extremely hungry and needs to eat right away.

What You Are Teaching

Your baby will learn to enjoy exploring, and will also learn self-reliance and independence skills with this game. The mess is a small price to pay for all that!

What You Need

To play this game, you just need a few things—a baby-size spoon, a jar of jelly, crackers or toast—and being okay with making a mess!

9+ months Explore the House Game

This game is especially fun for your baby if you do it in a room that she doesn't visit often, or in a new location, such as a friend's house.

How to Play

Let your crawling or walking baby lead you around a new area or room. As she makes her way around, follow her and comment on what you see. Don't interfere with where she goes too much—except in the case of danger—and let her show you around.

Where and When

When you visit a new place—or just go to a room in your house that your baby doesn't get to enter very often—you can play this game. You'll want to make sure you're in a safe and trusted environment before letting your baby loose, so you may want to do some exploration of your own first.

What You Are Teaching

By encouraging your baby to see what's what in a new environment, you show her that she's capable of exploring and figuring things out on her own—independence skills that will help her later in life.

What You Need

For this game to be a success, you need a new space to explore (check it out ahead of time) and, as always, close supervision.

9+ months Explore Outside Game

We tend to corral our babies in playpens or on blankets when we're outdoors, but sometimes they just need the chance to roam around to explore and see what they can find.

How to Play

Let your baby show you around the great outdoors. Follow his lead and let him wander around and explore what's out there. To get him started, you might put a few of his favorite toys in various places that he can see. He'll zoom off to investigate and start to interact with the outdoors.

Where and When

This game is best played outdoors during the day, when the weather is mild.

What You Are Teaching

By letting your baby set the pace, you encourage his independence and exploration skills.

What You Need

For this game, you'll need a safe (preferably relatively flat) outdoor location, such as your backyard or a park, and some mild weather.

9+ months Grab the Spoon Game

When your baby starts grabbing at the spoon when you're feeding her, it means it's time to get her in on the feeding act!

How to Play

Let your baby hold her spoon to feed herself with it. Offer her small amounts of food—it's less overwhelming and also less messy. Also give her finger foods so she can feed herself, even if she doesn't manipulate the spoon very well.

Where and When

Because this game is messy, it's best played at home at mealtime or snacktime.

What You Are Teaching

Your baby will learn independence and self-reliance skills as she tries to feed herself. She will also have to develop fine motor skills to get the food from the spoon or the table to her mouth.

What You Need

For this game, you need a baby-size spoon, food to eat with a spoon (such as oatmeal), and finger food to offer when your baby can't quite get the spoon to her mouth.

Brainy Baby

Don't worry about the mess your baby creates in the "Grab the Spoon Game." (Imagine how annoyed you'd be if every two seconds while you were trying to do something, your mom wiped your face.) When your baby is doing more playing than eating, take that as a signal she is full and the meal is over.

9+ months Pick One Game

Babies definitely have preferences, and this game allows them the opportunity to express those preferences. It also let your baby feel like he's helping you, which is enjoyable for him.

How to Play

As you go through your daily activities, let your baby make choices (when you don't care about the outcome). For example, at breakfast, say to him, "Milk or juice? You pick one." Let him indicate which one he wants and put the other one away. You can also ask for his help at the grocery store. Show him two packages of cheese, for instance, and ask him to pick one. If he doesn't indicate a choice, say, "This package is less expensive, so let's get it" or "I like the taste of this cheese better, so let's get it." That way, you model how you make decisions.

Where and When

This game can be played anytime throughout the day as you're going about your daily activities. You can play it at home, at the store, or at the park—anywhere (and anytime) there are choices to be made.

What You Are Teaching

This game helps your baby learn decision-making skills—especially if you model decision-making behavior. It also helps your baby learn self-reliance, because he is allowed to choose instead of having everything decided for him.

 What You Need

For this game, you simply need to be aware of choice-making situations, and be willing to let your baby make choices.

 **Brainy Baby**

Offering more than two choices can be overwhelming for a baby, so when playing the "Pick One Game," limit the variety of choices until your child is older—around preschool age (or even older).

6+ months One Spoon for You and One for Me Game

A good time to introduce this game is when your baby starts developing an interest in feeding herself. This game helps build a variety of skills.

 **How to Play**

You and your baby should each have a spoon. Give your baby a bite to eat first to get things started. Then say, "Mommy's turn!" and you take a bite from your own spoon. Then let your baby hold her own spoon, and say "Terry's turn!" and guide the spoon into her mouth. Repeat the process of turn-taking until the meal ends, or for as long as your baby stays interested in the game.

 Where and When

Because of the potential messiness of this game, you'll want to play it at home, during mealtime or snacktime.

 What You Are Teaching

Because you're encouraging your baby to feed herself, you're showing her self-reliance skills. You're also modeling them by taking your turn. By the same token, you're teaching turn-taking skills.

What You Need

You'll need two baby-safe spoons for this game, plus food that you and your baby will both eat.

 # You Try First Game

Sometimes we know our babies too well—we anticipate all of their needs and give them everything they want. We're their caretakers, so this is natural. But babies also need to learn how to figure out how to do things on their own, and this game helps them develop that skill.

How to Play

When your baby needs help doing anything, say, "You try first," and encourage him to try. If he's reaching for a toy and makes a sound of frustration, don't just hand him the toy. Say, "You try first," and encourage him to reach for the toy. If he isn't successful, move the toy closer and say, "You try first" again.

Where and When

You can play this game anywhere and anytime throughout the day. In fact, you can play the game whenever you remember to do it!

What You Are Teaching

By showing your baby you believe he can do it, you're encouraging independence and self-reliance skills. By making him give it a try first, you're showing him the importance of persistence.

What You Need

For this game, you just need to be aware of situations in which your baby needs your encouragement to "try first." As always, you will want to make sure your baby is using baby-safe toys and objects.

Show Me Game

This game encourages independence and self-esteem by letting your baby lead the way.

How to Play

When your baby does something new, or performs an activity you've been encouraging her to do, say, "Show me how you did that!" Not only does repetition help her remember new skills, but she'll be delighted to involve you in her new endeavors. As she shows you, perform the task yourself so that she sees you imitating her; this helps validate what she's doing.

Where and When

Whenever your baby does something new on her own, play this game to encourage her. It can be done anywhere at any time.

What You Are Teaching

By encouraging your baby to do new activities, you're building her self-reliance skills. By asking her to repeat the new activities, you are helping her master them and learn the value of persistence.

What You Need

To play this game, you just need to be aware of when your baby does something new independently.

Creating a "Room" of Baby's Own Game

In this case, the "room" can be a cupboard or a box—anything that your baby knows he has complete access to. Knowing that he is allowed to play with anything in his "room" and that he has control over it gives him a sense of independence.

How to Play

Create a space for your baby in the rooms you spend most of your time in. For example, in the kitchen, you could devote a cupboard to your baby so that while you're preparing meals, he can play with objects in "his" cupboard. Remind him, "Here's Stephen's cupboard. Go ahead and play, Stephen!" Having a space of his own will keep him occupied while you're trying to get other chores done, and it will help keep him from digging into your cupboards (though you'll want to install child safety locks no matter what)!

Where and When

This game is best played at at home, anytime—especially when you need to get chores or other work done so your baby can be safely occupied with his own "work." It can also be appropriate at other places your baby visits for long periods of time, such as a grandparent's house or a home office.

What You Are Teaching

By giving your baby his own space and encouraging him to play, you're helping him develop his independence skills. Because he'll be able to explore the "room," you'll also help build his physical development as he manipulates the objects.

What You Need

For this game, you need to set aside a "room." This could be a cupboard, box, or set of shelves—a specific area that can be just for your baby. You'll also need toys and playthings to go in the "room."

6-9+ months Who's a Big Girl/Boy Game

Praising your baby encourages her to continue her exploration and development of self-reliance skills.

How to Play

Show your approval and praise your baby whenever she shows she's proud of herself for accomplishing a new task or doing something independently. Say, "Natalie is a big girl! Look at Natalie feed herself!" Give a specific reason for your praise; this encourages her to continue working hard to develop her skills further.

Where and When

You can play this game anywhere, anytime your baby does something new, independently.

What You Are Teaching

By praising your baby for her efforts, you help her learn the value of independence and self-reliance.

What You Need

For this game, you simply need an awareness of when your baby accomplishes tasks independently.

 **Brainy Baby**

Though your baby is striking out on her own and wants to do things for herself, she also needs reassurance and a connection to you. That's why praise is important at this stage, as are games and activities that you do together.

9+ months What Should Baby Wear Today Game

Like the "Pick One Game," use your baby's clothes in this game to help him learn to communicate his preferences.

 How to Play

In the morning, say to your baby, "What should Adam wear today?" Offer him a choice of two items—for example, a blue shirt and a red shirt. Say, "Which one?" Give him a moment to respond. Take any sort of gesture or attempt to speak as him communicating his preference. So if he grabs for the red shirt, say, "Adam wants to wear the red shirt today" and put it on him. While he may have been more interested in grabbing than choosing, over time, he'll understand what's happening and participate more fully.

 Where and When

This game is fun to play at home when you're helping your baby get dressed in the morning.

 What You Are Teaching

By involving your baby in the process—even though he may not quite understand what you're doing at first—you're encouraging decision-making and self-reliance skills in your baby.

What You Need

For this game, you need only the usual clothing choices you have in your baby's dresser.

 # What Should Baby Do Today Game

This game allows your baby to participate in the process of deciding what to do and encourages her to express what she desires. You'll be modeling your decision-making skills in order for her to learn how to do this herself.

 How to Play

Offer your baby a few choices of what to do next throughout the day. Ask, "Would you like to pet the dog or read books?" Show her the choices and let her communicate her decision to you. Model your decision-making process as well: "Our dog wants attention. See her wag her tail? Let's pet the dog first, then read books."

 Where and When

This game is fun to play anywhere and at various points during the day when you're deciding what to do next.

 What You Are Teaching

By offering choices and modeling how you pick, you're teaching your baby decision-making skills.

 What You Need

All you need is a willingness to involve your baby in decisions throughout the day, and choices of familiar activities to offer her.

The Least You Need to Know

- By creating opportunities for your baby to explore, you'll encourage a love of learning.

- Your baby will learn many independence skills by imitating you.

- Self-reliance skills depend on exploration, persistence, and learning by doing.

- Your baby has preferences, and letting her communicate them to you helps her become more independent.

- By modeling your decision-making skills, your baby will learn how to make his own choices.

12

Imitating and Pretending Games

In This Chapter

- ◆ Teaching your baby how to imitate others
- ◆ Moving from imitation to pretend play
- ◆ Showing your baby how to play with and manipulate objects
- ◆ Developing your baby's motor and social skills through imitating and pretending

Imitating and pretend play helps your baby learn how to think, sort through what's real and what's not, and imagine what it's like to be someone else. Imitating others is also how he learns about the world and how to interact with it.

Pretend play allows your baby to be in charge of what happens, which helps build confidence. As your child becomes a toddler and then a preschooler, these skills will help him learn the ropes of social interactions. In this chapter, we show you games that help encourage your baby to imitate and pretend.

Patting Game

Younger babies like to pat objects with their hands, and this game builds on that tendency to encourage them to imitate what you're doing.

How to Play

Gently touch your baby's back and say, "Mama pats Taylor." Then put his hand on your back and say, "Taylor pats Mama." Show your baby a favorite toy and say, "Mama pats the stuffed bear." Encourage him to do the same. Pat another toy and count the number of pats you do. Be sure to use only very soft, gentle pats.

Where and When

You can play the patting game anytime, anywhere. Once your baby learns the game, you can encourage him to pat other loved ones when they visit or when you visit them.

What You Are Teaching

This game encourages your baby to develop imitation and motor skills.

What You Need

No special equipment is needed for this game, just a gentle touch and watchful eye to make sure your baby doesn't pat too hard.

Brainy Baby

You can play the "Patting Game" with board books, too. Several popular books, such as *Pat the Bunny* by Dorothy Kunhardt, are made with textures and fabrics that your baby will enjoy touching. You can pat the bunny or pet the cat and encourage your child to imitate you.

12+ months Do What I Do Game

In this simplified version of "Simon Says," you encourage your baby to imitate you, which she'll enjoy doing. If you have older children, have them join in and play the game as a family.

? How to Play

Sit with your baby and say, "Can you do what I do?" Touch your nose and say, "Mama touched her nose." Then guide your baby's hand to her nose and say, "Diane touched her nose." Then touch the top of your head, rub your belly, touch your toes—whatever actions your baby is able to imitate. Sing a made-up song or rhyme as you play the game.

Where and When

Play this game at home when your baby is attentive to you (and others) and what you're doing.

What You Are Teaching

Your baby is developing imitation and social skills by playing this game with you and others.

What You Need

Again, no special materials are required for this game, just play-time with your baby.

6-9+ months Open and Shut Game

If you've ever opened your purse, backpack, diaper bag, or other bag in front of your baby, you know he's curious about what's inside and how the bag works. This game lets him explore opening, shutting, putting in, and taking out, and will give him extra enjoyment because he'll think he's acting just like you do.

? How to Play

Put a few small toys or baby-safe objects in an old purse or backpack. Open the purse, saying, "Open!" Pull out the toys and show them to your baby, then put them back in and say, "Shut!" Offer the purse to your baby and let him open it, take out the toys, and shut it. He may be more interested in taking out than putting in at first, but you can show him how it's done.

Where and When

This is a great game for your baby to play anywhere at any time, because you can bring along a purse or backpack wherever you go. Just make sure not to put special things in it that you wouldn't want to lose.

What You Are Teaching

Your baby is learning how to manipulate objects by having something of his own to open and close, and things to take in and out. He is also imitating you and gaining those skills as well.

What You Need

This one is easy, because it just takes an old purse (and who doesn't have one of those!), a backpack or other container that your baby can open and shut, plus a few simple objects to put in it. Be sure to change out the objects from time to time.

 Dress Up Dolls and Animals Game

For this game, find clothing that's easy for your baby to manipulate, such as hats and skirts with self-fastening tape closures instead of buttons and snaps.

How to Play

Give your baby a doll or stuffed animal and some easy-to-put-on clothing. Show her how the clothing can be taken off and put back on the doll or animal. At first she will be interested only in taking the clothing off, but eventually she will start dressing up her dolls and animals.

Where and When

This is great game to play at home with your baby's toys during playtime.

What You Are Teaching

This game teaches your baby motor skills and aspects of pretending.

What You Need

Use your baby's dolls and stuffed animals and some clothes and accessories for them, such as shirts, pants, and hats. Or use some old baby clothes that your baby has grown out of; she may enjoy dressing her dolls and animals in her old clothes.

12+ months Dressing Up Game

Although at this age, your baby won't play dress-up the way a toddler or preschooler will, he will still enjoy experimenting with hats, shoes, bags, and jewelry. Boys as well as girls enjoy trying on simple-to-wear items.

How to Play

Gather a collection of simple-to-use dress-up clothes and accessories in a box. Put a hat on your head, and then put a hat on your baby's head. Go look in the mirror to see what you look like. Comment about the hats you are wearing. Add a cape, jewelry, bags, shoes, and so on, talking about what you're wearing and what you look like. Remember to supervise your baby when he's dressing up.

Where and When

Play dress-up at home during playtime.

What You Are Teaching

Pretending and self-awareness skills are what your baby learns when playing dress-up.

What You Need

No need to run out and buy anything new for this game; your baby will likely be perfectly fascinated with what's in Mommy's or Daddy's closet. Simple dress-up objects like hats, purses, bags, a cape made from a length of fabric, and jewelry (for example, plastic Mardi.Gras beads) are all great for playing dress-up.

Brainy Baby

Take photos of your baby playing the "Dressing Up Game." Put them in a photo album and talk about them with your baby. "Look, there's Jimmy in a big hat!" Your baby will find the photos fascinating, and they'll help develop his self-awareness.

9-12+ months Sweep the Floor Game

Your baby will want to help you with your chores, and sometimes you can easily assign her a task—see the next game, "Helping Around the House Game." But other times the tools are too big for her to use, so this game allows her to imitate you by using her own tools.

How to Play

Give your baby a small broom and encourage her to help you sweep the kitchen floor. A play mop, tool bench, and other such toys can help her feel like she's participating in the chores that you're doing.

Where and When

At home when you are doing chores or working around the house is the best time to play, because your baby will want to do what you are doing.

What You Are Teaching

This is an ideal game to teach imitation and pretend play skills. It also teaches your baby about the activities of daily living.

What You Need

This game works best with child-size items such as a broom, vacuum, toolbox, and other household tools.

 Helping Around the House Game

Babies like to help around the house and do whatever you're doing. Letting your baby contribute makes him feel like a valued member of the family. This game doesn't require child-size tools, and your baby actually helps.

 ## How to Play

Encourage your baby to help you with your daily activities around the house. Demonstrate the techniques first and then give him a shot. It will take a while for him to master any of the skills, but give him plenty of opportunities to try.

For example:

- Your baby can help you carry in lightweight groceries and put them away.

- At mealtime, your baby can help you cook by stirring and pouring.

- He can set the table and carry dishes to the table.

- He can wash the table after the meal is over.

- He can take laundry out of the hamper to help you sort the wash, and put his socks away in a drawer when the laundry is done.

Over time, your baby will start using these skills in pretend play.

 ## Where and When

Play this game at home whenever you are doing chores where your baby can help.

 ## What You Are Teaching

This game teaches your baby imitating skills and gives him confidence.

 ## What You Need

You shouldn't need anything special other than what you already have for your daily routine and chores.

12+ months Putting Away Baby's Toys Game

Although it's usually easier and faster to do it yourself, get your baby involved in cleaning up her own messes. Not only does she enjoy helping, but it teaches her how to be responsible for herself—and this is a big step toward independence.

 ## How to Play

Make sure that you have easily accessible places for your baby's toys to be put away—for example, a cupboard, a toy box, or a set of low shelves designated for your baby's belongings. When it's clean-up time, tell her, "Let's clean up your toys." At first you will have to give her directions: "Put the red truck on the shelf like this." Over time, she will be able to do it without your direction. You can sing a song while you're cleaning up to make it more fun.

 ## Where and When

At home, when it's time to pick up and clean up. Also, this game carries over very well when you're visiting friends or relatives and want to pick up after yourselves at their house.

 ## What You Are Teaching

Your baby is learning both imitation skills and a sense of responsibility.

 ## What You Need

You won't need special materials for this game; it's just a matter of including your baby in picking up after herself.

Dr. Larry's Little Known Facts

Though you should always encourage your baby to clean up and take responsibility for her belongings, studies show that children who do well in school have mothers who allow them to explore, rather than restricting them so they don't make such a mess, and who relax their housekeeping standards to accommodate for their baby's need to explore and dump everything on the floor. So give your baby the opportunity to make a mess, and then teach her how to help clean it up.

12+ months Animal Tea Party Game

Although your baby will be older before he initiates this game or can play it by himself, it can be a fun activity for you to show him how to play.

How to Play

Gather a few of your baby's stuffed animals or dolls and sit them around a small table or arrange them on a blanket spread out on the floor. Ask your baby to help you set the table with a play tea set or cups. Be sure to give yourself and your baby a cup. Pretend to pour tea (or milk or juice) into all of the cups. Describe each of the steps to your baby as you do them, giving him a chance to respond to you and to help you.

When everything is ready, sip from your cup and say, "Mmm! That's yummy tea." Help the animals drink their tea, too, encouraging your baby to do the same.

Where and When

At home or outside in the yard or in the park on a nice day is a great time for this game during playtime.

What You Are Teaching

This classic game teaches your baby pretend play skills.

What You Need

You will need your baby's animals or dolls, a play tea set or child-sized cups and plates, and a small table or blanket.

3-6 months Clapping Hands Game

Your young baby loves to master physical movements, and this game helps her use her hands with your guidance. By imitating you and interacting with you, she'll learn an important skill.

How to Play

Sit with baby on your lap. Clap your hands together and say, "Mama claps her hands!" Then gently clap your baby's hands together and say, "Bianca claps her hands!" Sing a song, clapping as you say the words, and help your baby clap along.

Where and When
This is an easy game to play anywhere at any time.

What You Are Teaching
By clapping with your baby, she learns both imitation and motor skills.

What You Need
All you need are your hands.

12+ months Let's Pretend We're Lions Game

Babies enjoy animals, and this game lets them think about the characteristics of different animals while encouraging action and movement so that they don't get bored.

How to Play
Show your baby a picture of an animal, such as a lion, to help him visualize what you're doing. Say, "Let's pretend we're lions." Roar like a lion and encourage him to roar, too. Get on your hands and knees and pretend to walk like a lion, encouraging your baby to do the same. Talk about the characteristics of the animal you're pretending to be—"Does it have a tail? Yes, it has a tail, and soft fur."

Where and When
This game works well at home or anywhere when you are having playtime.

What You Are Teaching
By acting like a lion or other animal, you are teaching pretending skills as well as analytical skills.

What You Need
Having a storybook with pictures of animals or sturdy cards with pictures of animals is great for this game.

 **Feed the Doll Game**

Babies love to mimic what you do for them, and this game lets them do just that.

 **How to Play**

Say to your baby, "Time to feed the doll [or use the doll's name]!" You can also use a stuffed animal or a baby-friendly action figure. Sit the doll up and pretend to feed it with the spoon. Say to your baby, "Jacqui's turn!" and give her the spoon to feed the doll or stuffed animal. Talk or sing the way you do when you're feeding your baby, and use the same cues: "Looks like your doll is getting full!" and "Don't throw the spoon!"

Where and When

Play this game at home or anywhere at playtime.

What You Are Teaching

This game teaches your baby the basics of pretend play. Since you're modeling the behavior, she will learn how to use her imagination. Plus, this game encourages building fine motor skills necessary to control the spoon to feed the doll.

What You Need

You'll need your baby's favorite doll or stuffed animal, a baby-safe spoon, and pretend food, such as empty boxes of pudding or play food.

Brainy Baby

If appropriate, use the same doll for both the "Feed the Doll Game" and the "Give the Doll a Bath Game." This way, your baby can see the relationship between feeding the doll (and the doll getting "dirty") and giving the doll a bath to get her clean. If you're using a stuffed animal for the "Feed the Doll Game," you can always pretend to clean the doll afterward.

12+ months Give the Doll a Bath Game

Boys and girls can play this game—if your boy doesn't have a doll, a baby-safe plastic action figure that can be immersed in water works just as well.

How to Play

Fill a plastic tub about half full with water and add a small amount of soap or bubble solution to the water. Give your baby a washcloth or sponge and encourage him to wash the doll. Or let your baby wash his doll while he is taking his bath. The doll can be dried with a dry washcloth.

Where and When

Play this game in the bathtub at bathtime or outside when your baby is playing with water.

What You Are Teaching

This game mainly teaches your baby imitation skills, but it also encourages the self-care skill of washing up.

What You Need

You should already have what you need on hand: a doll that can get wet, a sponge or washcloth, and a plastic tub or container if you're not playing in the bathtub.

12+ months Washing Toys Game

Toys can get grimy during play, so encourage your baby to take care of her toys by washing them.

How to Play

Fill a plastic tub about half full with water and add a small amount of soap or bubble solution to the water. Encourage your baby to wash a collection of water-safe toys, scrubbing to get them shiny and clean and then drying them thoroughly.

Where and When

Play this game outside during water play or inside in the bathtub—preferably not when your baby is taking a bath so she's not bathing with dirty toys. Be sure to supervise this game closely since it involves water.

What You Are Teaching

This game teaches imitation skills because your baby likely watches you wash dishes, clothes, and other items throughout the day.

What You Need

You likely have the items for this game on hand: plastic toys that can be immersed in water, a washcloth or sponge, and a plastic tub or container.

6-9+ months Hand Puppet Game

Most babies enjoy playing with toys while interacting with you. This simple game allows you to model some imitation and pretend skills that your baby will need as he grows older.

How to Play

Put on a hand puppet show for your baby by having two hand puppets interact with each other. They could sing, dance, talk to your baby, and give him hugs. Offer him the chance to put a puppet on his hand and encourage him to play as you're playing.

Where and When

This is a great game to play anywhere at any time, because hand puppets are so easy to carry with you—and babies love them.

What You Are Teaching

Playing with hand puppets promotes imitation and social skills.

What You Need

You need two or more hand puppets to play this game. You can also make them using felt.

Baby Beware

Be sure that any hand puppet you use in the "Hand Puppet Game" is baby-safe, with no small parts that can be pulled off and swallowed. Your baby is likely to chew on his puppet friend!

9-12+ months Draw What I Draw Game

Babies love to scribble on paper. This game helps them begin to understand the purpose of scribbling, though they'll be older before they have the motor skills to draw realistically.

 ### How to Play

Take a crayon and draw a simple shape on the paper. Name the shape: "Daddy drew a circle." Give a crayon to your baby and invite her to draw the same shape: "Can Maddy draw a circle?" Then encourage her to draw something. Ask her what it is, even though she may not be able to express it. Give it your best guess and try to draw it on your paper. Take turns being the leader.

 ### Where and When

This is an easy game you can play anywhere at any time.

 ### What You Are Teaching

This game is another way to teach imitation and motor skills.

 ### What You Need

Crayons and paper are all you need.

The Least You Need to Know

◆ Imitation is one of the most important ways your baby learns about how to interact with the world around him.

◆ Your baby wants to feel like an important part of the family, and letting her help you makes her feel needed.

◆ Your baby will develop necessary social skills through imitation and pretend play.

◆ Your baby can learn to take responsibility and care for his possessions at a young age through imitating you.

13

Showing Love and Helping Your Baby Understand Emotions

In This Chapter

- Showing how emotions are communicated through expressions and actions

- Naming emotions so your baby can identify what she's feeling

- Sharing your feelings of love and affection with your baby

- Building a strong foundation of love and trust with your baby

By naming the emotions that your baby—and other people—are expressing, you'll help your baby understand how to identify her own emotions, as well as how to express her needs without having to burst into tears. (Though we can pretty much guarantee that she'll continue bursting into tears for a while yet.)

In this chapter, we describe games and activities you can use to show your baby how much you love her. We also show you how you can help your baby learn to understand emotions—hers and other people's.

3+ months **Why Is Baby Crying Game**

By helping your baby learn the names for his feelings, you can help him learn to identify his own emotions and share them with you and others.

How to Play

Once your baby gets past the newborn stage, you probably have a pretty good handle on why he's crying when he cries. So when you hear him cry, go to him and ask, "Why is Brad crying? I bet Brad has a wet diaper and feels uncomfortable."

If you're not sure why he's crying, ask him: "Is Brad wet? No, Brad's diaper is dry. Is Brad tired? But Brad just had a nap and he seems wide awake. Is Brad thirsty? Should we try some milk?" As a young baby, he won't be able to respond to your questions, but he will learn to put names to his feelings.

Where and When

This is an easy and important game to play anytime and anywhere.

What You Are Teaching

You are letting your baby know that emotions have names and that communicating his emotions can help him get his needs met.

What You Need

All you need is patience and kindness when your baby is crying for unknown reasons.

3-6+ months What Makes Baby Feel Better Game

This game helps your baby make the connection between expressing an emotion and getting her needs met. This encourages her to communicate what she wants and needs.

How to Play

When your baby expresses a need, describe what you're doing to help her feel better. For example, you may say, "Simone is crying! Simone must be hungry. Mama is going to feed Simone and then Simone will not feel hungry." Eventually your baby will make the connection between communicating her needs and getting them met. She will also learn that instead of crying, she can name her feeling or need with the understanding that it will be met. Of course, she'll still use crying for the next 18 years or so, but she'll also learn to use her words!

Where and When

Play this game anywhere when your baby is expressing a strong emotion.

What You Are Teaching

Your baby is learning that communicating her feelings helps caregivers give her what she needs.

What You Need

Again, just some patience, kindness, and positive communication with your baby is all you need.

Dr. Larry's Little Known Facts

Very young babies don't actually feel fear. They have to have memories and the ability to anticipate what could happen for fear to occur. Around six months, most babies start having stranger anxiety (dislike of unfamiliar people) and separation anxiety (unwillingness to be separated from their primary caregivers). At this time babies can begin to anticipate an unpleasant event. This is when a baby could start developing a concept of fear.

6+ months Happy or Sad Game

Talking about emotions, particularly being happy or sad, helps your baby identify what he is feeling and learn to communicate it to you and other caretakers. Show him how by talking about your own emotions.

How to Play

Talk about your own emotions with your baby throughout the day. Say, "My friend just yelled at me. That makes me sad. Would Joey be happy or sad if someone yelled at him? I bet Joey would be sad, too."

You can also talk about the emotions you see in books and on other people's faces. For example, you may say, "In the book, Sally got a dog. Would Joey be happy or sad if Sally got a dog?" If your other children are having an argument, you may say, "Your sisters both want the same toy. Do they sound happy or mad to you?"

Where and When

This game can certainly be played anywhere at any time, because we experience different emotions all day long. When your baby is having a strong emotion, try to get him to tell you how he's feeling.

What You Are Teaching

This game teaches your baby the names of emotions and the situations that may cause certain feelings.

What You Need

Awareness of feelings (your own and your baby's) is all you need.

9+ months Name the Faces Game

This game helps your baby identify emotions as shown in people's facial expressions. Because most babies are very interested in people's faces, this game will catch her interest.

How to Play

Show your baby a picture of a face with a clear expression on it. Say, "That person is smiling. See how her lips curve up? She looks happy." Then point to another picture, describing it: "He looks sad. See how his lips are turned down? He is crying. See his tears? This man is sad." You may want to start with simple emotions, such as happy, sad, mad, and scared. As your baby gets older, you can introduce more sophisticated emotions, such as confused and bored.

Where and When

Naming faces is great to do at home using books or magazines during playtime or reading time. It's also great to play when you're out and about, when you're seeing lots of different faces.

What You Are Teaching

Your baby learns that people communicate emotions through their facial expressions.

What You Need

Books with pictures, magazines, and photos are great items to use to find expressive faces.

 Mimicking Baby's Face Game

As we learned in Chapter 12, babies learn a lot through imitation. In this game, you're imitating your baby's facial expressions. By mirroring his expressions, he can see what you see on his face and begin to understand what he is communicating to you with his body (facial) language.

How to Play

When your baby is happy, mad, or sad, describe his expression. You may say, "Charlie is frowning." Then put an exaggerated frown on your face. Then describe what emotion you think he feels, based on what his face is showing. "Charlie's frown makes me think that Charlie is mad. Is Charlie mad? Can Charlie say why?" This helps him see that his face is communicating his emotions. Don't forget to imitate him when he's happy and smiling, too!

Where and When

Mirroring of facial expressions can be done anywhere when you're playing and spending time with your baby. It's particularly useful to do when he is expressing a strong emotion.

What You Are Teaching

You are showing your baby that facial expressions communicate emotion.

What You Need

All you need to effectively play this game is to feel, and be, a little clownlike.

Fingertip Kisses Game

This gentle activity makes a nice "good night" game, but it can be played anytime you want to show your baby some affection.

How to Play

Rock your baby in a dim, quiet room. Say or sing words of affection, including your baby's name, such as "Daddy loves his baby Jena." Then kiss your baby's fingertips. Say the words again and kiss her cheek, her toes, whatever she seems to like and enjoy. Name her body parts as you kiss them. As your baby gets older, she'll enjoy asking for a "nose kiss" or a "fingertips kiss."

Where and When

Play this game at home anytime, but before naptime or bedtime is ideal.

What You Are Teaching

You are showing your baby you love her, and how love is expressed.

What You Need

All you need are kisses!

Together Time Game

Birth +

Our days are constantly interrupted with the needs and demands of the outside world. By setting aside some special time with your baby, you help create a strong bond between the two of you.

How to Play

Set aside 15 minutes or half an hour every night to interact with your baby with no outside distractions. A good time to do this is usually right before bedtime. Don't take (or make) phone calls during this time, don't check email on the computer, and don't answer the door or have visitors. Just spend some quiet time with your baby. Establish a routine (for example, see the "Goodnight, Stuffed Bear Game" in Chapter 10) and follow it.

Where and When

Spend this time together at home at bedtime as regularly as possible.

What You Are Teaching

This game demonstrates to your baby that interacting with your baby is important to you, and that you love him.

What You Need

This activity takes what we all enjoy to have with loved ones—uninterrupted time.

Reconciliation Game

6+ months

Even the most even-tempered, best-intentioned person can get stressed with a baby. This game helps you and your baby forgive each other for the challenges of the day and share some love.

How to Play

Take a deep breath and describe to your baby what happened that made you (and your baby) upset. For example, you may say, "Nicole has been crying all morning. Daddy tried to understand but couldn't. Then Daddy used his loud voice, and that made

Nicole and Daddy feel bad." Give your baby a hug and say, "Let's forgive each other for what happened." Hold your baby and say and think peaceful and loving thoughts until you are both relaxed and calm.

You may find that hugging your baby and describing what's happening or what you're feeling can head off a loss of temper in the first place.

Where and When

Make reconciliations anywhere you and your baby have had a stressful experience.

What You Are Teaching

This game shows your baby that people who love each other also forgive each other, and that sharing loving affection is calming.

What You Need

The ability to let things go and not hold grudges is essential for forgiveness and reconciliation.

Dr. Larry's Little Known Facts

A newborn's smile is the result of neurological activity—or the result of passing gas. By about three months, your baby will develop a "social smile"—that is, a voluntary smile that she uses around people who interact with her and make her feel good. This is the beginning of her journey to understanding emotions and how to communicate them to those around her.

Birth + — Write Your Wish Game

This game involves all the people who love and care for your baby, and it makes a treasured memento to share as he's growing up.

How to Play

Mark a journal or notebook with the phrase, "What I Wish For" and your baby's name. Hand visitors to your house a pen and ask them to write their wish for your baby. Have them sign and date their wish. For relatives and friends who live far away, ask them to send or e-mail their wishes, and paste or tape them into the book. As your baby grows up, read the book to him and tell him who the people are and what they want for him.

Where and When

Play this game at home when you have friends and loved ones over to visit, or take the journal with you when you're visiting other people or traveling.

What You Are Teaching

This is a great way to show your baby how he is loved by many people, and that people have loving hopes and dreams for him.

What You Need

This activity is easy to assemble with a journal or notebook, a pen or markers, and some glue or tape.

9-14+ months Create a Treasure Box Game

The treasures you gather with your baby in the "Gathering Treasures Game" from Chapter 9 will be even more cherished in a special treasure box you and your baby make yourselves.

How to Play

With your baby, decorate a box or container with stickers, paint, or markers. Label it with her name and the words "Treasure Box" and fill it with treasures you and she have collected. For a bigger container, you could put your baby's handprints or even footprints on it (see Chapter 6, "Handprint Game").

Where and When

This is a great activity to do at home during playtime.

What You Are Teaching

Your baby learns that sharing memories of fun experiences bonds family members together.

What You Need

These materials aren't hard to scare up: a cardboard or plastic box or container (an empty, dry egg carton works, too), paint, stickers, and/or markers. Be sure to use baby-size, nontoxic materials for this game.

 # Guess How Much I Love You Game

This simple game can be used to show your baby how much you love him no matter where you are and what you're doing. In fact, strategic use of this game can head off baby temper tantrums and Mommy melt-downs, too.

 How to Play

Whenever you are feeling affection for your baby—or need to remind yourself or your baby of your affection—ask your baby, "Guess how much I love you?" Then stretch your arms out wide and say, "This much!" and then reassure your baby that you will love him no matter what. You can also play this game after a stressful experience with your baby, to remind him that you love him even if you've had to scold him.

 Where and When

This is certainly one to remember to use anywhere at any time to express your feelings of love for your baby, or diffuse an upsetting situation.

 What You Are Teaching

Your baby is learning how much you love him, no matter what.

 What You Need

Use your arms and your imagination to tell your baby how much you love him.

 **Brainy Baby**

Read the book *Guess How Much I Love You* by Sam McBratney with your baby and assure him that you love him that much, too.

Birth + Tender Touches Game

Physical affection reassures your baby as much—or more—as verbal "I love you's" do. This game encourages loving touches between a baby and her caregivers.

How to Play

Tell your baby you love her while giving her a gentle hug or a butterfly kiss. Or touch her cheek and tell her how much she means to you. The combination of touch with verbal affirmation is a powerful message of love.

Where and When

Touch and tell your baby how much you care everywhere you go, at any time. Babies never get tired of hearing and feeling love from their caregivers.

What You Are Teaching

You are showing your baby how much you love her and love being with her.

What You Need

Kisses and hugs are all you need.

6-9+ months What I Wish Game

Sharing your dreams and hopes for your baby reinforces the bond the two of you share, and it gives your baby a sense of how much you love him.

How to Play

Tell your baby what you wish for him. You may say you wish your baby to grow up strong and wise, or that he lives happily ever after, or whatever particular dreams and values you want to pass along to him. In the beginning, your baby will only hear your warm voice, but as he gets older, he'll begin to understand what you are saying.

Where and When

Share dreams with your baby at home during quiet time, when you are spending time together.

What You Are Teaching

This game shows your baby that you love him and want good things for him—that you have values you want him to share.

What You Need

This game only requires the expressing of dreams and encouragement.

Birth + What I Love About You Game

While your baby will always appreciate your loving words, being specific really makes a difference in how appreciated and loved your baby feels.

How to Play

Don't just tell your baby you love her—say what it is about her you love, and why! "I love Lucy's laughter! I love Lucy's sweet chubby cheeks!" She'll understand that you love her for herself, and identifying some of the things you love about her makes her feel special.

Where and When

It's always a good place and time to tell your baby why you love her so!

What You Are Teaching

This is another way to show your baby that you love and value her.

What You Need

Use complimentary and descriptive language with your baby about what you love about her.

Brainy Baby

Researchers are beginning to believe that if a baby doesn't reach certain emotional milestones, she may have difficulty with other cognitive tasks, such as acquiring language. Some of these milestones are developing a social smile (at about 3 months), displaying emotions like surprise and frustration (at about 6 months), and showing interest in what is interesting to other people (at about 10 months).

Birth +

Collect the Postcards Game

This is a fun game to play if your baby has loved ones who live far away, or if you have to travel without him for some reason. It reminds him that even if he can't see you, you're thinking about him and love him.

How to Play

Send a collection of postcards (self-addressed and stamped is a nice touch) to loved ones who live far away. Ask them to write brief notes to your baby on the postcards and mail them every now and then. When you receive them, read them to him, describe whom they're from, and put them in a journal or notebook.

When you travel without your baby, purchase postcards and write a note to your baby, then mail it home. Have your baby's caregiver show the postcards to him. Then, with his help, put them in the journal when you return.

Every now and then, get out the journal and read the loving notes to your baby.

Where and When

Send postcards to friends and relatives anytime of the year, perhaps during "down time" from birthdays and holidays in order to provide something fun to fill in other times of the year. Look through the journal at home at any time, or set special times when you and your baby get it out to look at it.

What You Are Teaching

This game reassures your baby that he is loved.

What You Need

Just gather together some postcards, envelopes (for sending the postcards), stamps, a journal or notebook, and some glue or tape.

 **Sharing What You Love with Your Baby Game**

6-9+ months

Involving your baby in all aspects of your life makes her feel loved and appreciated. Besides, you never know—you might turn her into a life-long Dodgers fan!

 How to Play

Let your baby join you in some of your own hobbies and recreations. If you like to bowl, bring your baby to the bowling alley and show her around. An older baby may enjoy rolling a ball down the alley with your help. If you like baseball, take her to a game. If you like to paint, show her some of your work and sit her down with a canvas and some nontoxic paints. Babies love to be involved in all aspects of their parents' lives, and this game helps your baby feel a part of your life, as well as loved and appreciated. It also gives you a chance to share your passion for a particular hobby or pastime with her.

 Where and When

The right place to share what you love with your baby depends on what you love to do, so it may be in your workshop or garage, at a baseball or football game, in the garden or kitchen … the possibilities are endless. Include your baby when you will be in a position to involve her and spend quality time with her during the activity.

 What You Are Teaching

Being together doing your favorite hobbies teaches your baby that you enjoy certain activities and want to share them with her.

 What You Need

Your own hobbies and interests are what you need for this game, along with the ability to involve her.

The Least You Need to Know

- Your baby needs a caregiver's help in learning how to understand her emotions.

- Emotions are communicated not only by actions, such as crying, but through facial expressions as well.

- By naming the emotions your baby is feeling, you're validating him and giving him information he needs to understand why he's feeling the way he does, and what he can do about it.

- Babies need to know they're loved, and they feel it in a variety of ways, including gentle touch.

- Sharing your emotions with your baby helps her understand how to recognize and communicate her needs back to you.

Part 5

Stimulating Your Baby's Sensory Development

Babies learn about the world through their five senses, but often parents just focus on developing two of them—hearing and seeing.

In this part, we'll share games and activities you can use to help your baby develop her senses of smell, taste, and touch in addition to sight and sound, and open up new worlds to her.

Relating to Your Baby Through Smell and Taste

In This Chapter

- ◆ Exposing your baby to the world of taste and smell
- ◆ Comforting your baby with scent
- ◆ Understanding how others, including animals, use their senses of taste and smell
- ◆ Encouraging your older baby to try new tastes

The sense of smell is the first sense to develop. From a very young age, your baby can use smell to differentiate among people. Babies also explore the world through their sense of taste—which is one of the reasons they like to put objects in their mouths!

In this chapter, we show you games to help your baby develop two closely related senses, the sense of smell and the sense of taste. By encouraging your baby to explore the world through the senses of taste and smell—safely and with guidance—you're also helping your baby develop important listening, language, thinking, motor, and social skills.

12+ months Name the Smell Game

Your baby may not be able to name different smells yet, but he'll particularly enjoy smelling foods and learning from you and others how to recognize and, eventually, name and describe them. In this game, you will be naming the smells so your baby can learn them.

How to Play

Show your baby different containers of food. Lift one to your nose, take a deep sniff, and say, "That smells like lemon." Then offer your baby a chance to sniff. He'll probably also want to taste and chew, and that's okay. As your baby gets older, you could have him cover his eyes and guess the smell without looking. At mealtime, you can play this game with anything that you're cooking that has a distinct smell.

Where and When

Name smells at home when you're preparing a meal or a snack.

What You Are Teaching

Your baby is learning how to distinguish among smells and the words for different smells.

What You Need

This game is easy to play with whatever you have in the fridge or pantry, using small containers or bowls of distinct-smelling foods, such as tuna, cheese, fruit, and cookies (especially when they're baking).

12+ Name the Taste Game
months

Your baby will be a little older before she'll be able to say the names of the tastes, but still encourage her to try when she's younger so she can learn them. Use concrete words to help her learn how to describe tastes, such as tart, sour, sweet, salty, tangy, and bitter.

How to Play

Show your baby different containers of food. Take a taste from one of them and describe how it tastes to her. Offer her a taste and ask her what she thinks of how it tastes. Do the same with the other foods. Let her touch and smell the food, too. It's also fun to use facial expressions, because that goes along with learning what feelings different tastes are associated with.

Where and When

This game can really be played anywhere you are eating, whether it's at home, at mealtime or snacktime, or out to lunch in a park or restaurant.

What You Are Teaching

Your baby will gain the ability to distinguish among tastes, the words associated with different tastes, and even the willingness to try new tastes.

What You Need

All that's needed are foods with a variety of different and distinct tastes, such as a tart apple, a sweet orange, and salty pretzels or crackers.

12+ Teeny Tiny Taste Game
months

Babies can be overwhelmed by the presence of too much food on their plate or in their bowl, with the result that they reject it all. Even what seems to an adult to be a small helping can seem like a great deal of food to a baby. This game encourages your baby to try new tastes without overwhelming him.

How to Play

At your baby's mealtime, introduce him to a new taste. Put a tiny dab on his spoon (or his thumb) and say, "Here's a teeny tiny taste of marmalade." Give yourself a teeny tiny taste and encourage him to eat his. Don't ask or expect him to eat more than the little taste unless he specifically indicates that he wants to.

Where and When

This is a great game both at home at mealtime and snacktime. It's also fun in a restaurant or at a friend's house, when your baby is exposed to food you may not normally fix at home.

What You Are Teaching

Presenting your baby with new tastes promotes his exploratory skills and willingness to try new things.

What You Need

New foods for your baby are all you need—likely items you already have on hand.

> **Dr. Larry's Little Known Facts**
>
> Studies have shown that newborns prefer sweet tastes. They'll happily suck on a bottle of sweetened water, but will cry or refuse something bitter or sour. Because of this preference, caregivers often offer only fruits and other sweet foods when they introduce solids to their babies. However, this makes babies less inclined to try salty or sour foods like vegetables when they're introduced later. Try offering solids that have both sweet and sour characteristics (in a mild form), such as sweet potatoes.

12+ months Smell the Food Game

Use this game to explore the world of food through your baby's sense of smell. It requires no special preparation or tools, just awareness as you walk through the world.

 ### How to Play

Play this game when you're out and about and you happen to smell food, such as french fries being cooked at a restaurant or popcorn being popped at a movie theater. Take a deep sniff and ask your baby if she can smell that yummy smell. Give her a chance to respond, then tell her what you think it is. If it's appropriate, give her a small taste of the food she smells.

 ### Where and When

This is a great activity anytime you're at the grocery store, the mall, a restaurant, or an outdoor market—anywhere you smell food!

 ### What You Are Teaching

Your baby is learning to distinguish smells and the words used for different smells.

 ### What You Need

All you need is an awareness of when you enter a restaurant or area with a strong food smell; take a moment to notice and talk about it.

 # What Do Animals Eat?

9+ months

Babies are curious about animals and enjoy learning about how they live. This game teaches your baby about what animals eat. You can also use it to talk about how you think the various foods might taste.

 ### How to Play

Show your baby a picture of a familiar animal, or give him a stuffed animal to play with. Say, "What does a horse eat? A horse eats oats." You can also describe what you think the food would taste like, or compare it to what your baby eats. "I bet the horse's oats taste like oatmeal."

 ### Where and When

You can play this game at home, anytime your baby is willing to look at pictures of animals or play with stuffed animals.

What You Are Teaching

This game helps your baby understand that animals have senses, just like he does.

What You Need

For this game, you can use pictures of familiar animals—such as ones you'll find in a simple storybook—or you can use stuffed animals or baby-safe plastic or wooden figures.

0-12+ months **Knowing Mama's Scent**

Even tiny babies are able to tell the difference between their mother's scent and other people's. Even at a week old, babies show a definite preference for Mama's smell. This game helps reassure your baby through smell when you're not there.

How to Play

Keep a cloth against your body as you nurse or feed your baby—this will be the "scent cloth." The fabric of the cloth will absorb your smell over time. Leave the cloth with a caregiver when you're not available for your baby. The cloth will reassure the baby through its scent. (But remember that loose cloths and blankets should not be left with a baby unsupervised or placed in her crib without supervision.)

Where and When

Keep a cloth close to you when you're holding your baby as much as possible so it picks up your scent. Leave this cloth with your baby when you're not with her.

What You Are Teaching

Having a cloth or blanket with your scent on it reassures and comforts your baby through the sense of smell.

What You Need

Use a receiving blanket, unused diaper, or burp cloth.

9-12+ months Guess the Smell Game

Because your baby doesn't have much expressive language until he's older, it's hard for him to ask you questions about what he's experiencing. Often we'll tell our babies about what they see and hear, but we forget to tell them about what they smell. This game helps us answer some of the questions our babies can't ask.

How to Play

When you're going through your daily activities, be aware of all the smells around you. Share your awareness with your baby. For example, when you're outside and you smell flowers, you may sniff the air and say, "I smell something good! Can you guess what it is?" Give your baby a chance to respond. Then say, "I smell flowers!" Ask your baby if he smells it, too.

Where and When

Smells are everywhere, so you can play this game really anywhere, at any time.

What You Are Teaching

This game teaches your baby scent identification and words to use to describe smells.

What You Need

All you need is a sense of smell!

Brainy Baby

Your young baby finds your scent soothing. Older babies find other scents soothing, too. You can use these scents to help your baby relax. For example, spraying a little bit of lavender in your baby's room gives him a pleasant, relaxing smell to fall asleep to.

12+ months Give It a Dip Game

Babies love dipping food into sauces—maybe because of the mess it makes! But allowing your baby to dip away can encourage her to try new foods.

How to Play

Offer your baby some foods she hasn't tried before, or some that she's tried but didn't seem to care for. Ideally these foods should be something she can pick up with her hands. Give her a bowl of dipping sauce that she likes, such as ketchup or a creamy salad dressing. Encourage her to dip her food in it and try eating it that way.

Where and When

It's okay to give your baby "dip" with any meal, when the food is suitable for it. It may be easiest to try this at home first so your baby gets used to the idea of dipping her food.

What You Are Teaching

Your baby gains a willingness to try new tastes and is exploring her senses through eating new foods in new ways.

What You Need

Prepare some new foods that you'd like your baby to try, and have some dips such as low-fat ranch (or other) dressing, ketchup, or yogurt.

12+ months You Taste Some If I Taste Some Game

Because babies love to imitate their caretakers, you can often get them to try new foods by trying them yourself first. Your baby will be a lot older before he catches on to what you're doing and stops falling for it.

How to Play

Show your baby a new food you'd like to introduce in his diet. Ask him, "Will Shane try some if Daddy tries some?" Take a bite and describe what it tastes like. Then offer it to your baby. He may refuse at first, but take another bite and try again.

Where and When

This will be a game you play quite often at mealtime, and it's easy to play anywhere. You may even find yourself using this game to help keep your baby focused on dinner!

What You Are Teaching

This activity is teaching your baby a willingness to try new tastes and lets him explore the use of his senses.

What You Need

You will need a willingness to eat what your baby is eating—so it goes both ways!

12+ months Stop and Smell the Roses Game

In this game, you'll stop and smell the roses ... and the rocks, grass, trees, leaves, and anything else of interest that you encounter.

How to Play

Take your baby on "a smelling walk." This could be around the house, in the backyard, at the neighborhood park, or even at the zoo. Stop at everything your baby seems interested in and see if it has a smell (of course, be sensible and first make sure it's safe to smell and touch). Encourage your baby to sniff, too. Use concrete words to describe what you're smelling, or relate it to something your baby already knows, such as "That flower smells like Mama's perfume."

Where and When

Take a walk around your home or in a park during the day, so your baby can see what she's smelling.

What You Are Teaching

Your baby learns to associate smells with objects, and you are encouraging her exploration of the world.

What You Need

All you need are a stroller, a safe place to take a walk, and a variety of objects to smell.

 **How Does This Animal Taste Things Game**

Babies are curious about animals, and this game helps babies understand their own taste buds through thinking about how animals use their sense of taste.

 **How to Play**

Show your baby a picture of an animal, such as a dog. Ask him, "How does the dog taste things?" Give your baby a moment to respond, then say, "The dog uses his mouth to taste things." Point to the dog's mouth. Then point to your baby's mouth and say, "Tim tastes things with his mouth, too!" Discuss other animals the same way.

 Where and When

Play this game anytime you're reading books together or having some playtime. Another opportunity for this game is when you visit the zoo.

 What You Are Teaching

This game teaches babies that animals have senses, too. By learning this, babies begin to understand their own senses.

 What You Need

Pets; pictures of animals, either on cards or in books or magazines; or a trip to the zoo.

 **How Does This Animal Smell Things Game**

This game encourages your child to use her imagination and her knowledge of the world around her to identify how animals use their sense of smell.

How to Play

Show your baby a picture of an animal, such as an elephant. Ask her, "How does the elephant smell things?" Give your baby a moment to respond, then say, "The elephant uses his nose to smell things." Point to the elephant's nose, and describe how long it is, and what else the elephant uses it for. Discuss other animals the same way.

Where and When

Play this game at home when you're looking at books or magazines, or when you take a trip to the zoo.

What You Are Teaching

This game teaches babies that animals have senses, too. By observing the animals, your baby learns to understand her own senses.

What You Need

If you have a pet, you can use your pet to play this game. Otherwise, you can use pictures of animals, such as ones you'll find in a storybook, or you can take a trip to the zoo.

12+ months What Does Mommy Have Game

Babies love to imitate what their caregivers are doing. In this game, you can use your baby's love of imitation to encourage him to try new foods.

How to Play

Eat a meal at the same time as your baby. Put some of the same things on your plate as what's on your baby's plate, but make one thing different. Show it to your baby. Ask, "What does Mama have?" Take a bite of it and tell him how good it is. Offer him a bite. Chances are he'll be interested because you have something on your plate that he doesn't have on his.

Where and When

Play this game at home at mealtime or snacktime. After trying it at home a few times, try it when you're out to eat, too.

What You Are Teaching

This game encourages your baby's willingness to try new tastes and promotes imitation skills.

What You Need

You just need a variation on what you're feeding your baby, one that he'll likely want to try.

12+ months Try, Try Again Game

Babies usually need to be exposed to new tastes several times before they're willing to try and like the new taste. This game reminds you to keep offering your baby chances to try a taste instead of assuming her preferences are firm and will never change.

How to Play

Offer your baby a new food, such as mashed sweet potatoes. If she refuses or spits it out, don't insist. Put it away. A few days later, introduce her to the mashed sweet potatoes again. If she still doesn't want it, don't insist. Try again a few days later. You can rotate the foods you're trying with her. Eventually she will give the new food a taste and may eventually learn to like it.

Where and When

Play this game at home at mealtime or snacktime. You can try it when you're eating out as well.

What You Are Teaching

Your baby is learning how to try new tastes.

What You Need

All you need are some baby-friendly foods that are new to your baby.

 Which Food Tastes Like That Game

You don't have to have an actual taste test with real food to talk about how food tastes. By actively discussing and describing how different foods taste anytime during the day, you'll encourage your baby to learn about his own taste and to explore the world around him through them.

 ### How to Play

Show your baby a picture with various kinds of food on it. Ask him to point to the apple (or whatever is pictured). Give him a chance to respond, though he may not. If he doesn't, point to the apple and say, "That's an apple." If he does point, say, "Yes, there's the apple." Then say, "An apple is crisp and sweet." Ask him to point to other foods, and describe what they taste like.

 ### Where and When

You can talk about your sense of taste easily anywhere, anytime. The grocery store is great place, as well as a restaurant or farmer's market. Remember to use simple descriptions your baby will understand.

 ### What You Are Teaching

Your baby learns the names for different kinds of foods, begins to understand the words that describe the tastes, and starts to use symbolic thinking.

 ### What You Need

All you need are pictures of food on cards or in books or magazines. You could also take a trip to the grocery store.

 ### Brainy Baby

Your baby's senses of smell and taste help him decide what's dangerous and what's not. In fact, researchers theorize that babies are "programmed" to prefer sweet foods because they're less likely to be poisonous than bitter tastes.

 Smell the Pictures Game

This game is a variation on the "Describe How Food Tastes Game," this time exploring the sense of smell.

 ## How to Play

Show your baby a picture of something with a distinct smell and ask her what it smells like. Then give her some concrete words to use: "This is a trash can. It smells stinky."

 ## Where and When

Scents are easy to describe anywhere, anytime.

 ## What You Are Teaching

Your baby is learning the names for different kinds of smells, as well as symbolic thinking.

 ## What You Need

A ride in the car to see different smelly things, or pictures of things that smell on cards or in books or magazines.

The Least You Need to Know

- Your baby has a preference for sweet things, but with persistence and some games, you can encourage him to try a variety of foods.

- Exploring the senses of taste and smell helps your baby develop important skills.

- You can use the sense of smell to comfort your baby.

- By describing tastes and smells to your baby, you'll give her the language she needs to understand them.

- Babies are curious about how others use their senses and perceive the world.

15

Stimulating Visual Development

Your baby will develop cognitive skills, such as memory and matching, along with visual skills, by playing games that encourage him to find an object. In this chapter, we give you guidance on how to play these types of games.

We also provide games and activities to do with your baby to help him develop his sense of sight. Your baby will learn how to control his visual motor skills, such as tracking and focusing, by following objects you move around. We also show you some ways to help your baby learn how to distinguish among similar objects.

0-18+ months Choosing Appropriate Books

Reading aloud to your baby encourages listening skills, builds vocabulary, helps develop attention span and memory, and familiarizes her with the idea of reading to get information. Babies also learn by looking at illustrations and hearing you talk about what you see. It's important to choose appropriate books for your baby's age.

0 to 3 Months

At this early stage, your baby will probably be more interested in hearing your voice than in interacting with a book. Books with nursery rhymes or songs and simple black and white illustrations work well for this age group.

3 to 6 Months

As your baby gets older, he will want to interact more with the book, so be sure the book can stand up to his exploration. He is likely to grab and chew a book. Touch and feel books, which appeal to the senses, can be a good choice, as are books with text that describes what's in the illustrations. Simple visual designs and bold colors are good for this age group.

6 to 12 Months

At this stage, try books that contain pictures and words about daily routines and books that label everyday objects and body parts. Books with flaps to manipulate or buttons to push are fun for this age group. Illustrations can also be more complicated.

12 to 18 Months

For older babies, books that show prepositional words, such as "above," "below," "in," and "out," help them understand these concepts. Books with active verbs, such as "running," "playing," "eating," and "sleeping" also appeal to this age group. So do books that tell simple stories with a beginning, middle, and end. Sing-along and rhyming books are also fun for this group. More complex illustrations allow you to ask questions to draw your baby's attention to the pictures. You can ask, "What's happening in the picture? Where is the dog?"

0-6+ months   See the Mobile Game

Young babies haven't learned to control their visual motor skills, so hanging a mobile helps them learn to look at something of interest and track it as it moves. Young babies are also learning *visual discrimination*, and mobiles help them explore differences among objects.

How to Play

Hang a mobile above your baby's crib, out of reach. Blow on it to make it move, or move it with your hand so your baby watches what it does. Talk about the objects as you touch the mobile, describing them to her. You can change or add to the mobile every now and then to add interest.

Where and When

Hang the mobile at home over your baby's crib, and play with it when she is awake and lying in her crib.

What You Are Teaching

Looking at the mobile helps develop your baby's visual motor skills.

What You Need

You need a simple mobile in bold colors or black and white, with several different objects hanging from it.

> **BABY BABBLE**
>
> **Visual discrimination** is the ability to see even small differences in the size, shape, and color of different objects. Developing this type of comparison and contrast skill is necessary for your baby to understand the world around him.

> **Baby Beware**
>
> Always make sure that a mobile is secure, out of reach, and baby-safe. Mobiles can be a real danger as babies get old enough to stand up in their crib and pull them down.

3+ months See the Sock Game

Babies love to wave their hands and grab their legs. This game takes advantage of that and encourages your baby to use his eyes and his arms or legs together.

How to Play

Put a brightly colored sock on your baby's foot or hand. Show him the sock. He'll want to explore it by waving his hand or foot around, grabbing for it, and staring at it.

Where and When

This is a great activity to do whenever your baby is alert.

What You Are Teaching

This activity teaches your baby to focus and aids in the coordination of sight and motor skills.

What You Need

You just need a colorful baby sock . Have a variety of different colored and patterned socks to keep this activity interesting for your baby.

Birth + Follow the Toy Game

If your baby has older siblings, they can play this game with her. It's a simple and fun way for older children to interact with young babies.

How to Play

With your baby in your lap, or on her back in her crib, show her a toy. Then move it around, up and down, side to side, nearer and farther. Start slowly so she can keep up, then move faster. You can also add sound effects to make the game more fun and keep her attention.

Where and When

Play this game anytime your baby is alert and playful.

What You Are Teaching

Your baby's visual motor skills, such as focusing and tracking, are being exercised in this game.

What You Need

Use a brightly colored or black and white baby toy to play.

 Follow the Buzzing Bee Game

This simple game is a lot of fun for both you and your baby. It will bring a smile to your lips to see him so captivated as he follows the "bee" with his eyes.

How to Play

Holding your baby, move your finger around so that his eyes follow it. Make a "bzzz" sound, like a bee, to attract and keep his attention. Let the bee land on your baby's cheek with a gentle stroke. Then let your baby try. Guide his hand into the air, making a "bzzz" sound for him, and put his finger on your cheek.

Where and When

This game is fun and easy to play anywhere—at home, in the park, in a waiting room, or anyplace you can sit or lay with your baby.

What You Are Teaching

This game teaches your baby visual tracking and imitation skills.

What You Need

This game just takes a little initiative and creativity from you.

Dr. Larry's Little Known Facts

Very young babies see best when objects are 7 to 9 inches away from their face. They are near-sighted, and objects much farther away appear blurred to them.

6+ months Flashlight Game

Babies never seem to tire of watching light dart around a room. As your baby gets older, she'll want to be in charge of the flashlight.

How to Play

In a dim room, turn on a flashlight and move the light over the walls and ceiling. Encourage your baby to follow the movements of the light with her eyes. You can move the light around on her toys, telling her what you're doing. "The light is on Beth's truck. Now it's on Beth's bed."

Where and When

This is a fun activity to do at home before bedtime.

What You Are Teaching

By following the light, your baby is gaining visual tracking skills.

What You Need

You need a flashlight and a dark room to play.

3+ months Silly Faces Game

This game capitalizes on your baby's love of human faces to stimulate his vision and encourage him to interact with you.

How to Play

With your baby in his crib or on your lap, look at him and make a silly face. Scrunch your nose, stick out your tongue—anything that changes your expression. He'll watch what you're doing, and may even try to imitate it!

Where and When

You can play this game anywhere and anytime your baby is alert and wants to play with you.

 ### What You Are Teaching

This game helps your baby develop visual discrimination skills as he watches your face change. It also helps him learn about human faces and encourages him to imitate you.

 ### What You Need

All you need are yourself and the willingness to be a little silly.

 # A Few of My Favorite People Game

This game builds on a baby's visual preference for human faces.

 ### How to Play

Take clear, uncluttered photos of the faces of loved ones. Show them to your baby and watch as she examines the faces. Tell her about the people she is seeing, even though she won't understand everything you're telling her right away.

Babies also love pictures of babies, so you can entertain her by showing her pictures of babies from magazines or from your photo collection.

 ### Where and When

Play with the photos at home during playtime, or take them with you when you go to the park or visit loved ones for an activity to do while you're there.

 ### What You Are Teaching

This game builds on your baby's developing visual discrimination skills and encourages her interest in and love of human faces.

 ### What You Need

You'll need photos of loved ones. You can ask if they have favorite photos they're willing to copy and share with you, or you can have them pose for a photo session. You'll need a camera and the capability of printing the photos onto paper.

Look at That Game

Although you may find your surroundings old hat and don't really notice your environment anymore, it's all new and interesting to your baby.

 How to Play

Draw your baby's attention to interesting things in his environment. "Look at that! There's a squirrel by the front door!" Then describe what you see.

 Where and When

This is definitely an anywhere, anytime activity. Just take whatever is around you and think of it as totally interesting and fascinating.

 What You Are Teaching

This game teaches your baby observation skills and visual discrimination.

 **What You Need**

Just look around, that's all you need!

> **Dr. Larry's Little Known Facts**
>
> Babies don't see color until they're about four months old. This is why when you're playing games to stimulate a very young baby's vision, we suggest using black and white objects, or objects with highly contrasting colors.

What Does Baby See Game

With this game, your baby indicates what interests her, while you help her understand what she's seeing.

 How to Play

As you notice your baby looking at things in her environment, encourage her by playing this game. Say, "What do you see?"

Name the object. Describe it in a few simple words. If appropriate, bring it closer to your baby, or your baby closer to it, so she can see it more clearly.

Where and When

This is another anywhere, anytime game using whatever is around you.

What You Are Teaching

Your baby is acquiring observations skills and visual discrimination.

What You Need

All you need is whatever your baby is looking at and interested in.

6+ months Burst the Bubbles Game

This game is fun for older siblings, too, so you can make it a fun outdoor activity for the whole family.

How to Play

Blow some bubbles in the air and show your baby how to poke one and make it pop. Encourage him to catch one himself. If he can't, catch a bubble on the wand and hold it out for him to poke. Don't forget to wash his hands afterward.

Where and When

Blow and pop bubbles outside in the daytime. This game can also be played inside if you don't mind wiping up a little bit afterward.

What You Are Teaching

This game stimulates visual motor skills and eye-hand coordination.

What You Need

You need a jar of bubbles with a wand.

Who's in the Mirror Game

Babies love looking in mirrors, and with this game, they'll have fun exploring objects and their reflections.

How to Play

Sit with your baby in front of a mirror. Show her one of her toys. Tap its reflection in the mirror and ask, "Who's in the mirror?" Let her explore the mirror and the toys.

Where and When

Play this at home during playtime, when your baby is alert.

What You Are Teaching

You are helping your baby acquire visual discrimination abilities.

What You Need

All you need are a mirror and some favorite small toys.

Dr. Larry's Little Known Facts

In very young babies, their eyes don't work together or coordinate the images that they're seeing. Some researchers believe that babies see two images at the same time (whereas the brains of older children and adults combine the images they see in each eye into one picture). Babies begin to coordinate their eyes at about three to six months.

Peek-a-Boo Game

This game has entertained generations of babies. If a young baby can't see you, he thinks you've disappeared. This game helps him recognize that you're still there.

How to Play

Hold a diaper, receiving blanket, or even your hands in front of your face and ask, "Where's Mommy?" Then show your face, saying, "Here's Mommy!" or "Peek-a-boo! I see you!"

Where and When

This timeless game can be played anywhere at any time, and it's an easy game for other loved ones to play with your baby, too.

What You Are Teaching

Your baby is learning visual motor skills and object permanence.

What You Need

Just something to cover your face is all you need.

Birth + Wave the Scarf Game

This low-tech game helps your young baby gain control over her eye movements.

How to Play

With your baby on her back on the floor or in her crib, show her a scarf by hanging it above her head. Lower the scarf closer to her. Then lift it away. You can also wave it back and forth to encourage side-to-side eye movement and tracking.

Where and When

Play this game at home when your baby is content to be lying on her back.

What You Are Teaching

Visual tracking and visual motor skills are what your baby learn by moving objects around in her field of vision.

What You Need

Use a scarf, handkerchief, or other small piece of fabric.

Birth + Bird Watching Game

You can encourage a love of wildlife and at the same time stimulate your baby's vision with this game.

How to Play

Hang a birdfeeder so that you can see it from a window. Fill it with birdseed. When a bird stops by, show it to your baby. Describe the bird's color and what it looks like. As your baby gets older, he may like to help you fill the feeder. You can also find a book on birds at the library and use it with your baby to help identify the birds that visit your feeder.

Where and When

You can watch birds anywhere in the daytime, but starting out at home will help make this game more understandable to your baby. You can then play it in a park or other place where you can more closely monitor the birds.

What You Are Teaching

Your baby is gaining visual motor skills, such as focusing and tracking.

What You Need

You need a bird feeder and bird food in a place where you and your baby can easily see it.

12+ months Nature Walk Game

Most babies love to go for walks and experience the outdoors. This game encourages you and your baby to pay close attention to what you see.

How to Play

As you take a walk through the neighborhood, stop and look at the things you see. Count the number of legs on a spider and watch how its web catches flies. Describe the color of a butterfly's wings. As the seasons change, notice the changes in the landscape. The tree that was bare on your last walk might be beginning to show some leaves.

Where and When

Take a nature walk during the daytime, when your baby is awake and alert to her surroundings.

What You Are Teaching

Your baby is gaining visual motor skills and visual discrimination ability.

 ### What You Need

You'll likely want to have a stroller for the nature walk. You may want to bring along a little jar to put in bugs or leaves that you find along the way.

 Baby Beware

Signs that your baby may have vision problems include being uninterested in faces or brightly colored objects (at birth), not tracking objects (around two months), not seeming to see you from across the room, or not reaching for objects (around three months). Other problems you may notice at any time include not seeing objects unless they're held very close; turning or tilting her head to see an object; redness, swelling, or discharge around her eyes; cloudy appearance to her eyes; and lots of tearing or blinking or seeming sensitive to light. If your baby suffers any kind of eye injury, she should be immediately evaluated by her pediatrician.

 # 12+ months Create a Sticker Picture Game

Many older babies enjoy playing with stickers (don't forget to supervise) but need help peeling them. Peel back a corner of the sticker and let your baby do the rest, or place a sticker on your baby's finger and let him put it on the paper.

 ### How to Play

Give your baby a set of stickers and some paper and help him create a "drawing." He can arrange the stickers in whatever arrangement pleases him. You can also purchase sets of stickers that show everyday activities and use them to tell a story about your baby's day.

Where and When

Stickers are fun and easy to play with anywhere, during playtime or when you're waiting somewhere.

What You Are Teaching

This activity promotes your baby's visual motor skills and eye-hand coordination.

What You Need

Stickers, either permanent or removable, and paper or sticker books are all you need.

The Least You Need to Know

- As with any motor skill, your baby needs games and activities to learn how to use his eyes to focus on and track objects.

- Your baby can learn how to visually detect even small differences in the size, shape, and color of objects she interacts with.

- Reading aloud to your baby and helping him follow along in books from a young age strengthens his sense of vision and also helps him build language skills.

- You can show your baby how to interact visually—in a safe manner—with the world around her.

- Young babies respond more readily to simple designs and bold colors than to complex patterns and multiple colors.

Chapter 16

Stimulating Auditory Development

In This Chapter

♦ Helping your baby discover his sense of sound

♦ Showing your baby how to manipulate objects to make noise

♦ Encouraging your baby to look for the sources of sounds

♦ Teaching your baby the different characteristics of sound

♦ Appealing to your baby's innate love of human voices by singing

It's time to encourage your baby to make her own noises, and to listen to and understand the noises the world makes. In this chapter, we show you games and activities to help your baby explore the world of noises. Many of the games demonstrate how your baby can manipulate the environment to make noise, while others encourage your baby to learn where the sounds are coming from.

Your Biggest Fan

Whether you like (and have the ability) to or not, your baby loves to hear you sing no matter what. Your voice reassures your baby, and he's enchanted by the sounds that he hears.

Why Your Baby Responds to Singing

In every culture, mothers sing to their babies, which suggests that humans are programmed to sing to their little ones in order to stimulate their development.

The language centers of the brain are in the right hemisphere of the brain, while hearing music stimulates the left hemisphere. This suggests that listening to songs may play an important part in establishing important neural networks that will later help your baby put his thoughts and feelings into words.

What You Need

Your baby will probably like anything that you sing, but the classic baby songs, like "Rock-a-Bye-Baby" and "Hush, Little Baby" seem to have particular appeal because of their short verses, pleasant melodies, and simple lyrics. For most of the activities and games in this chapter, unless otherwise noted, what you need (in addition to some courage!) is to learn the tunes and lyrics to baby lullabies and rhymes. Visit your local library, music store, or go online to find a variety of music geared toward babies.

Birth + Bedtime Lullaby Game

Even if your singing makes the dog hide under the table, your baby will love listening to your bedtime lullabies. Sure, you can pop a CD in and let your baby listen to that, but she'd really rather listen to you.

How to Play

As part of your bedtime routine, softly sing a lullaby or two to soothe your baby to sleep. It can even be the same lullaby every night; your baby will like the repetition.

Where and When

Sing lullabies to your baby at home at bedtime or naptime.

What You Are Teaching

Listening skills and the routine of bedtime are key things your baby learns through lullabies.

What You Need

Learn the tunes and lyrics to some simple lullabies, and use a soft singing voice.

12+ months Loud and Soft Game

Your baby isn't born with an understanding of *voice modulation*—that is, controlling how loud or soft his voice is depending on the situation. This game helps him understand it and eventually learn how to control it. As he grows older, you can remind him when to use his inside voice (softer) versus his outside voice (louder).

BABY BABBLE

Voice modulation means controlling or changing the stress, pitch, or loudness of your voice. Babies and young children often have to be reminded of how loud or soft their voices are at any given time.

How to Play

Sing a song that your baby knows, starting loudly. Gradually lower your voice until you're whispering. Then make your voice louder again. Invite your baby to sing softer and louder. As your baby gets older, he can ask you to sing louder or softer.

Where and When

This game is great to play at home during playtime, when it's appropriate to use a louder voice.

What You Are Teaching

Your baby is learning voice modulation and listening skills.

What You Need

The courage to sing loudly is all you need!

12+ months High and Low Game

Just as your baby needs to learn about loud and soft voices, she needs to learn about tone, too. Your tone of voice tells your baby a lot about how you are feeling, even more than the words that you use.

How to Play

Sing a song your baby knows, starting in a high pitch (think shattering glass, and then bring it down a few notches). Gradually lower the tone of your voice until you're speaking in a deep, gruff "Papa Bear" pitch. Then make your voice higher again. Invite your baby to sing in higher and lower tones. As your baby gets older, she can ask you to sing higher or lower.

Where and When

This is another activity that's best to play at home during playtime so you can reach those high notes in private!

What You Are Teaching

Your baby is learning voice modulation and listening skills.

What You Need

The courage to hit some high notes is all you need!

9+ months Beep-Beep Game

Your baby probably discovered your nose when he was three or four months old. This game capitalizes on your baby's fascination with faces—namely noses.

How to Play

Tap your baby's nose and say, "Beep!" Then show him how to tap your nose. When he does it, say, "Beep!" Use different pitches for "Beep!" as you play the game. This game is usually good for giggles!

Where and When

This game is one you can more easily play in places other than at home, when you and your baby are feeling playful.

What You Are Teaching

This game teaches your baby cause-and-effect and about the fun of making noise.

What You Need

All you need is your nose!

6+ months Tap and Clap Game

Babies love to bang things. This game helps you show your baby different ways she can use her hands to make noise.

How to Play

Show your baby how to tap a bowl or box to make a sound. Clap in time with your baby's tapping. If she's curious about what you're doing, show her how to clap her hands together. As she gets older, you can show her how to combine taps and claps to make a rhythm.

Where and When

This is a great game to play in the kitchen on pots and pans, during playtime or after a meal.

What You Are Teaching

Your baby learns she can manipulate objects to make a noise, and the game helps her develop her listening skills.

Dr. Larry's Little Known Facts

Your baby will be about four months old before she begins to turn toward the source of a sound. Before then, she may startle or blink at a sound, but she probably won't try to look at where it came from yet.

What You Need

This game requires different objects that can be tapped or banged on, such as an overturned plastic bowl, pan, or box.

6+ months Bang the Drum Game

Your baby doesn't have to use a drum for this game. You can use any musical instrument that your baby can manipulate, like a tambourine or maracas.

How to Play

Offer your baby the opportunity to perform his own musical accompaniment when you sing. Give him a toy instrument and show him how to play it. You can sing a song while your baby plays his instrument, or you can both play instruments. Play recorded music or an appropriate music station on the radio to encourage his efforts.

Where and When

Play this game at home during playtime, unless you want to drive everyone at the store crazy!

What You Are Teaching

Your baby is learning he can manipulate objects to make a noise and is developing his listening skills.

What You Need

Have some baby-friendly musical instruments on hand, such as a toy drum or tambourine.

6-9+ months Listening to Music Game

This activity exposes your baby to different kinds of music. It's also a great way to introduce her to music that may be special or meaningful to her culture.

How to Play

Put on some music for you and your baby to listen to that has definite rhythms and beats, such as:

- ◆ **Flamenco**—Spanish music with acoustic guitar
- ◆ **Gamelan**—Indonesian music based on striking gongs
- ◆ **Merengue**—Dance music from the Dominican Republic and Haiti
- ◆ **Reggae**—Jamaican folk music
- ◆ **Rumba**—West Indian music
- ◆ **Salsa**—Latin dance music
- ◆ **Zydeco**—Cajun music

At first, just exposing your baby to different kinds of music is all you need to do. As your baby gets older, talk about what you hear, identifying the musical instruments as they play. Get a book from the library and show her pictures of the instruments she's hearing.

Where and When
Great places to listen to music together are at home, in the car, or at an outdoor concert or festival—just the two of you or with family and friends.

What You Are Teaching
This activity helps develop listening skills and teaches differences in sound and music.

What You Need
Just tune in to different radio stations or get recordings of different kinds of music to listen to.

6+ months Shake, Shake, Shake Game

By the time your baby is six months old, he'll probably be grabbing and exploring everything within reach. This game satisfies his need to explore while appealing to his sense of sound. If the toys you use make different sounds, so much the better.

How to Play
Give your baby a rattle and show him how to shake it. Offer him other toys that also make sounds. He'll be excited to try and discern the differences in the sounds he's hearing.

Where and When

This is an easy game to play anywhere, anytime, because these types of toys are highly portable.

What You Are Teaching

Your baby learns he can manipulate objects to make a noise and is developing listening skills.

What You Need

You need toys that make sounds when you shake them, such as rattles.

Baby Beware

Most babies have no problem with their hearing, but you can do some simple checks to make sure. If your baby is younger than 3 months, try clapping your hands behind him (so he doesn't see you). He should be startled by the sound. For a baby that is 4 to 6 months old, try calling his name and see if he looks for you. Around 6 to 10 months old, he should respond to his name and to familiar sounds, like his pet dog barking. When he's a little older (between 10 and 15 months), ask him to point to a familiar object in a book.

Always discuss any concerns about your baby's development with your pediatrician.

Birth + — Soothing Sounds Game

Your baby can be soothed by sounds just as she can be stirred up by them. This game helps you discover which sounds are most soothing to your baby.

How to Play

To find sounds that are soothing and calming to your baby, try singing lullabies, crooning meaningless words, or humming a cheerful tune. You may also want to explore CDs of lullabies, sounds of rain falling, or the rhythm of the ocean lapping against the shore, or buy a white noise machine. Notice which ones she responds to (and in what way), and use the sounds to help your baby calm down when she's upset.

Where and When

Play soothing sounds anywhere when you need to calm your baby down.

What You Are Teaching

Your baby learns listening skills and that music and sounds can be comforting.

What You Need

Try getting some CDs with lullabies or different types of soothing sounds on them, or a white noise machine.

3-6+ months Can You Find Mommy Game

In very young babies, the sound of your voice helps your baby learn *audio localization*.

How to Play

With your baby on the floor or being held by another adult, walk around the room while singing songs or talking to him. He won't look around for you at first, but over time he will try to figure out where you are by listening to the sound of your voice.

Where and When

Play this game at home when it's quiet so your baby can hear just your voice.

What You Are Teaching

Your baby is learning where sounds are coming from—audio localization.

What You Need

This game just requires your familiar voice.

BABY BABBLE

Audio localization is the ability to figure out where a sound is coming from. Babies need practice to figure this out, and to learn how to coordinate their vision with their hearing.

12+ months Piggy Bank Game

This game is as much about motor skills as about exploring sounds. Like many games you can play with your baby, it helps integrate her various senses and teaches her cognitive concepts, such as cause-and-effect.

How to Play

Cut a hole in a plastic lid from a container. Put the lid on the container. Show your baby how to put objects in the container through the slot. Show her how they make a sound when they land and when you shake the container. She'll get the hang of it soon enough. Remember to supervise her with this game.

Where and When

This is great activity to play at home or in the park during playtime.

What You Are Teaching

Your baby is learning cause-and-effect, how to manipulate objects to make noise, and motor skills.

What You Need

Use a clean, empty plastic container with a lid. You can use blocks or similar objects to poke through the slot, but make sure they are large enough not to pose a choking hazard.

6-9+ months Crinkle the Paper Game

Your baby will want to join in this fun by crinkling the paper, too. Let him have his turn at crinkling the paper—under your careful supervision, of course!

How to Play

Take a piece of paper and crinkle it in your hand, letting your baby listen to it. Take a different piece of paper and do it again. Your baby will enjoy exploring the paper and the sounds it makes.

Where and When

This one is easy enough to play in the car, at a restaurant, at friend's house, or just at home, anytime.

What You Are Teaching

This game teaches your baby listening skills and differences in sounds.

What You Need

Play with different kinds of paper—tissue paper, aluminum foil, or copy paper.

9-12+ months Music On, Music Off Game

Though you won't be playing musical chairs with this game, it's a great way to develop your baby's listening skills.

How to Play

Turn some music on and say, "On!" Then sing along to the music with your baby for a few moments. Then turn the music off and say "Off!" Repeat the process a few times. Eventually your baby will be able to tell you "on" or "off" for the music.

Where and When

This game is perfect to play in the car—a good distraction when she's cranky!

What You Are Teaching

This simple game helps your baby develop listening skills.

What You Need

You need music that appeals to your baby, and a radio or CD player.

6+ months What's That Sound Game

Your baby is intensely curious about everything that happens in his world. Loud noises startle him, and soft noises can catch his attention. With this game, you'll give him the words he needs to describe what he's hearing.

How to Play

Throughout the day, pay close attention to the sounds you hear. As adults, we tend to tune background noises out, but babies don't, and they're curious about what they're hearing. As you hear different sounds, label them for your baby: "Oh, I hear the birds singing outside! Let's go look" or "Those cicadas are loud tonight! Do you hear them?"

Where and When

Picking up on sounds is easiest at home or in a place that's not super noisy, where you can decipher particular sounds.

What You Are Teaching

Listening skills, sound identification skills, and labeling are all at work in this game.

What You Need

You need a relatively quiet environment and a certain sound being made loud enough for your baby to hear it.

Brainy Baby

Your baby should be screened for a possible hearing problem within the first month of his life. Although most babies have excellent hearing, some are born with hearing loss, which can affect their ability to learn and can cause language delays. With sophisticated new testing devices, screening tests can be done even the day your baby is born.

Dance to the Music Game

Babies love the movement of dance and will enjoy being whirled around in your arms as you listen to (and sing!) songs.

How to Play

Turn on some music and boogie with your baby! Hold her in your arms securely and twirl her around. If she's walking, hold her hands and sway to the music with her.

Where and When

At home, a friend's house, a party, a wedding—anywhere is a good place to dance together! Because this game is more energetic, it's not recommended to do right before bedtime.

What You Are Teaching

Listening skills are actually developed when your baby dances to music with you.

What You Need

All you need is some music to dance to—upbeat, soft, or classical, whatever suits you.

Find the Sound Game

Use a toy that makes quieter sounds for this game, or you could startle your baby and make him cry!

How to Play

Show your baby a toy that makes a noise and manipulate it so it makes its sound. Then move the toy back and forth, so your baby tracks the toy and the sound with his eyes.

Where and When

This is a flexible game to do anywhere, anytime.

What You Are Teaching

Your baby is learning audio localization and tracking skills.

What You Need

Use a toy that makes a quiet sound, such as a rattle or a squeaky toy.

The Least You Need to Know

- Your baby will be about four months old before she can turn toward the source of a sound.

- Play games with your baby to teach sound concepts such as "high" and "low" and "loud" and "soft."

- By encouraging your baby to listen to different kinds of music, you can help him develop a lifelong love of music and an appreciation of different cultures.

- Your baby will enjoy manipulating objects to make sounds.

- Babies have an innate love of human voices, and especially love having their parents sing to them.

17

Relating to Your Baby Through Touch

In This Chapter

- ◆ Understanding the importance of cuddling and touching your baby

- ◆ Using concrete words to describe how objects feel

- ◆ Encouraging your baby to explore the world through her sense of touch

- ◆ Showing your baby how touch can be comforting

- ◆ Exploring various textures through touch

Touch is one of the most important ways your baby learns about the world. By exploring touch, your baby builds body awareness and distinguishes among different objects in the world. As you pay attention to your baby's responses, you'll learn what types of textures your baby responds to and prefers.

In this chapter, we show you games and activities you can do with your baby to help him explore his sense of touch. In addition to encouraging your baby to touch things, we illustrate how your baby enjoys being touched by things—including you!

Birth + Comforting Surfaces

This activity can help your baby gain an awareness of the different parts of his body as he feels the warm material against his skin.

What to Do

Put warm, soft blankets on the floor for your baby to lie on. Let him lie naked on the sheet or blanket so that he can feel the material on his body.

Where and When

Use warm sheets and blankets at home, when you can take them right out of the dryer, at bedtime or playtime.

What You Are Teaching

Your baby learns body awareness and that touch can be comforting.

What You Need

You'll need soft sheets and blankets and a clothes or hair dryer to warm them up.

Birth + Small Circle Massage

While there is much to be learned about infant massage (check with your local birthing center or hospital for starters), you can do this simple version without special training.

What to Do

In a warm room, take off your baby's clothes except for her diaper (unless you don't mind cleaning up a mess!). Talk or sing to your baby as you massage her. Using a gentle touch, draw circles around her cheeks, torso, arms, and legs. The motion will help her relax.

Where and When

Massage your baby at home, before bedtime, or when she is upset to help her relax.

What You Are Teaching

Your gentle touch is showing your baby that touch can be comforting.

What You Need

All you need are your hands and fingers, and lotion if you prefer.

Birth + Gentle Squeeze Massage

This is another simple method of massage that your baby may enjoy. Remember to be very gentle! Some babies prefer a gentle squeeze to a light touch and find it more comforting. Think of it as the difference between someone patting you on the back for a job well done and giving you a big hug. Sometimes you may prefer one over the other.

What to Do

In a warm room with your baby naked except for his diaper, talk or sing to him as you give him a massage. Gently squeeze his arms, starting at the top and working your way down to his fingers. Do the same for his legs.

Where and When

Massage your baby at home, before bedtime, or when he is upset to help him relax.

What You Are Teaching

You are showing your baby that touch can be comforting.

What You Need

Use your hands and fingers, and lotion if you prefer.

Birth + Fingertip Brush Massage

Some babies find this very light massage appealing; others may find the light touch more annoying or ticklish than calming. Watch for how your baby responds.

What to Do

Make sure the room is warm enough for your baby to be naked and then take off her clothes (except for her diaper). Talk or sing to her as you use your fingertips to brush very lightly over your baby's skin in gentle strokes.

Where and When

Massage your baby at home before bed or when she is upset to help her relax.

What You Are Teaching

You are showing your baby that touch can be comforting.

What You Need

You need your fingers and a very gentle touch.

3+ months Tickle Game

This game helps your baby learn about various textures that can tickle, but it also requires you to pay attention to his responses. If he doesn't like the feel of something, stop the game and give him a cuddle. Then try a different texture later.

How to Play

Touch a ticklish object to your baby's skin, gently stroking him with it. Watch his response. Try another object and do the same thing. As he gets older, he will indicate his preferences and may even ask to play the game!

Where and When

Play this game at home during playtime.

What You Are Teaching

This game teaches your baby body awareness and how different things feel on his skin.

What You Need

Use objects with different ticklish textures, such as a feather or a piece of silk.

12+ months Textured Shapes Game

Most babies enjoy exploring different textures. If your baby dislikes how a particular material feels, that's okay. With familiarity, she may decide it's not bothersome to her. But never force her to touch something she doesn't want to.

How to Play

Cut different fabrics and materials into different shapes—squares, triangles, circles, and so on. Show your baby one of the shapes and tell her its name: "This is a square." Encourage her to touch it and say, "Feel the square." Be sure to supervise her so she doesn't put the materials in her mouth.

Where and When

Once you cut out the shapes, you can take them with you and pull them out to play anywhere.

What You Are Teaching

This game teaches your baby that exploring objects by touch can help her understand them.

What You Need

You need scissors and materials with different textures, such as fake fur, felt, and fine-grit sandpaper.

6-9+ months The Itsy Bitsy Spider Game

This game not only encourages a fun touch, it also teaches your baby to anticipate what's going to happen. As he gets older, he'll sing along with you.

How to Play

Sing the "Itsy Bitsy Spider" song. Use your fingers as the spider and have the "spider" crawl up and down your baby's arm in accompaniment to the song. At the end of the verse, tickle your baby. When he's older, he may want to play the spider, and you can take turns.

Where and When

This is a delightful, classic game you can play anywhere, anytime.

What You Are Teaching

You are teaching your baby touch can be fun and how to anticipate an action.

What You Need

You need to know the words and tune to the "Itsy Bitsy Spider" song, and have the courage to sing it!

3+ months Touch the Grass Game

This game is a wonderful way to introduce your baby to the great outdoors a little bit at a time, so she doesn't find it overwhelming.

How to Play

Bring your baby and a blanket outside. Spread the blanket on the ground and put your baby on it. Pluck a blade of grass and touch your baby's arm or leg with it. Gradually introduce her to the texture of grass by putting her hand on the grass.

As she gets comfortable with the feel of the grass, move her off the blanket and onto the grass. She'll probably try to pull the blades. Just don't let her eat them!

Where and When

Play this game outside in the daytime when your baby is alert and curious.

What You Are Teaching

This game teaches your baby that exploring the world by touch can help her understand it.

What You Need
You need a blanket that can be used outside.

 ## Belly Ball Game
This game grows as your baby does, with variations you can use as your baby gets older.

How to Play
Gently roll a light ball across your baby's torso. Run it up and down his legs. As he gets older, he'll want to grab it and kick it—that's fine! Encourage him to hold the ball while he sits up (this helps his balance). When he's able to sit unsupported, you can roll the ball to him and encourage him to bat it back.

Where and When
This game is safest to play at home, or outside in the yard or at the park on a blanket, when your baby is enjoying lying on his back.

What You Are Teaching
Your baby is learning body awareness and how objects feel.

What You Need
Use a small beach ball—nothing heavy.

 ## Playing with Paint Game
This game can get messy—but exploring the world often requires a bit of disorder. Try to contain the mess rather than stop it altogether, which limits your baby's experiences.

How to Play
You can let your baby play this game in her diaper, then plunk her directly into the bathtub afterward. Show your baby a jar of finger paint, then open it and pour it in a bowl. Demonstrate how to use a finger to paint on paper, and show her how to use the sponge (or a similar object) to paint on paper. Most babies enjoy playing with paint, but if yours doesn't, try again when she's a little older.

Where and When

Play with finger paint at home (your friends will appreciate that!) during playtime.

What You Are Teaching

This activity teaches your baby how to manipulate objects and how things feel.

What You Need

You need nontoxic finger paints, paper, plastic bowls for the paint, sponges and other objects your baby can use to paint with, and plastic or newspaper to protect the table.

3-6+ months What's That Feeling Game

We tend to focus on sights and sounds when we teach our babies about the world, and it's easy to forget that our babies are also feeling things that they don't understand. This game helps your baby understand his sense of touch.

How to Play

As you go through the day, remark on the things that touch you or your baby, so he can gain an understanding of them: "The wind is blowing right in my face! See how the wind is blowing those leaves along the street?" or "That railing is cold! We should have put on our gloves today."

Where and When

Noticing what you feel, no matter how small, and sharing it with your baby can happen anytime, anywhere—riding in the car, on a walk, at the store, in the kitchen, and so on.

What You Are Teaching

Your baby learns that exploring the world by touch can help him understand it.

What You Need

All you need is to notice different feelings you have that you can share with your baby.

 # Let's Get Wet Game

The object of this game is to experience water in a fun and safe way—other than taking a bath!

 ## How to Play

Get in your bathing suit and let your baby wander around in her diaper. Turn the sprinkler on a very low setting and encourage your baby to come near it, saying, "Let's get wet!" Let your baby set the pace. She may not want to get too close to the water or get too wet, though you can encourage her by doing it yourself. Most babies learn to enjoy getting wet. If you have older children, this is a great game to play as a family.

 ## Where and When

Play this game outside when the weather is warm.

 ## What You Are Teaching

Your baby learns body awareness and that exploring the world by touch can help her understand it.

 ## What You Need

Use a garden hose and a sprinkler or other outdoor water game, such as a small plastic waterslide or baby pool.

 # How Does It Feel Game

This game helps your baby put words to what he's touching so he can describe what he feels.

 ## How to Play

Put pieces of the different materials into the box so you can't see them. Place your fingers in the box and touch one of the materials. Tell your baby how it feels: "That feels smooth." You can then pull it out and show it your baby and let him touch it. Then encourage your baby to put his fingers in the box and touch one of the materials. As he gets older, he'll be able to describe the sensation himself, but when he's younger, give him the words he needs.

Where and When
This is an easy game to take with you and play anytime, anywhere.

What You Are Teaching
Your baby learns how to describe the things he touches.

What You Need
You need materials with different textures, such as fake fur, felt, and fine-grit sandpaper, and a box or container.

12+ months Wooden Letters and Numbers Game

This game isn't about forcing your baby to memorize the alphabet. It's a game that helps her become familiar with letters and numbers through touch.

How to Play
Show your baby some wooden letters and numbers. Make sure you use only materials that are sold as appropriate for your baby's age, because other kinds of wooden letters may pose a safety hazard. When you read a book, give your baby one of the letters and ask her to find it in the book. For example, if you give her a "b," find the "b's" in the book. You can use the numbers the same way.

Where and When
Play this game at home when you are reading or having playtime with your baby.

What You Are Teaching
This game shows your baby that exploring objects by touch can help her understand them.

What You Need
You need a storybook and baby-safe wooden letters and numbers (look for toys sold specifically for your baby's age).

 # Playing with Water Game

Most babies love to splash around in the water at bathtime, and it's important to let them do so. This game lets them play with water and learn about it.

How to Play

At bathtime, give your baby objects to play with in the water. Show him how to put water in a measuring cup and how to dump it out. He'll enjoy splashing and pouring.

Where and When

Play this game at home at bathtime, either before or after you've bathed him.

What You Are Teaching

This game teaches your baby that exploring the world by touch can help him understand it.

What You Need

You need a bathtub and objects that can be used to manipulate the water, such as measuring cups, funnels, and spoons.

The Least You Need to Know

- Your baby's sense of touch is one of the main ways he has of exploring the world around him.

- Encouraging your baby to explore her sense of touch helps her understand the world and how she feels.

- Your baby loves to be touched and held—and will continue to even as he becomes more independent.

- Talk about touch as you go about your everyday tasks with your baby.

- Give your baby the opportunity to get messy—that's how she'll learn.

Part **6**

Developing Your Baby's Physical Skills

Your baby has a huge task ahead of him—going from a helpless infant to an almost-toddler who can crawl and "cruise" (or maybe even walk independently). For him to get to where he's going, he needs to develop his motor skills.

In this part, we show you games and activities that will help your baby improve the strength, balance, and coordination he needs to develop both gross and fine motor skills. Next thing you know, he'll be skipping down the street ahead of you!

Building Your Baby's Strength and Balance

In This Chapter

- ◆ Developing body strength through physical games and activities

- ◆ Gaining body awareness and body control through feedback from the senses

- ◆ Learning to balance in order to sit and eventually stand, walk, and run

- ◆ Encouraging your baby to interact with the world in ways that increase her strength and balance

When teaching your baby how to build strength and improve balance, make sure you do not overtax her body. Many of the simpler activities, such as the stretching games, can be done with a newborn. Others require greater motor skills and are more appropriate for older babies.

In this chapter, we show you games and activities you can do with your baby to help improve her overall strength and balance. Remember, when playing games and doing activities with your baby, let her set the pace. If she doesn't like an activity, stop and try again later or try a different activity that she may enjoy more.

6+ months Lap Bounce Game

This game, which most parents play without even thinking about it, helps your baby develop the strength needed to stand and walk.

How to Play

Hold your baby so that he's standing on your lap. He'll bend and straighten his knees instinctively. In the beginning, you'll have to support him because his legs will buckle, but this is half the fun. As he gets stronger, he'll start to bounce on your lap.

When and Where

Your baby will love to bounce in your lap anytime, anywhere.

What You Are Teaching

You baby is gaining leg strength and balance playing this game.

What You Need

All you need is your lap and some strong arms!

3+ months Kick the Target Game

Babies love to kick—you won't have to teach your baby how! This game encourages your baby to kick with a purpose.

How to Play

With your baby on her back, hold up the target for her to kick. You may have to guide her feet the first few times so that she understands the point of the game. Once she figures out what you want, she'll be kicking the target without your help in no time!

When and Where

Play this game at home on the floor during playtime.

 ### What You Are Teaching

Your baby learns body awareness and gains motor skills.

 ### What You Need

All you need is a soft target for your baby to kick, such as a pillow, a stuffed animal, or your hands.

 **Dr. Larry's Little Known Facts**

Your baby's muscles develop from head to toe. First, she'll gain the strength to lift her head. Then her shoulders, arms, and back will develop. Finally, her hips, thighs, and calves will get their turn.

 **6+** *months*

Sitting Around Game

Encouraging your baby to do things from a sitting position will help him develop the strength he needs to sit unsupported.

 ### How to Play

When your baby is able to sit up with support, set him on the floor and surround him with pillows to help him stay upright. Then sit across from him and offer him toys to play with, preferably toys that require him to stay seated in order to play with them, such as a drum or a simple shape sorter.

 ### Where and When

Once your baby can sit up, you will play this game a lot, in different places at various times.

 ### What You Are Teaching

Your baby gains strength and balance.

 ### What You Need

You need pillows, rolled-up towels, or other soft supports, and sit-down toys to play with.

6+ months Airplane Ride Game

This game is fun for you and your baby. Your baby will learn a sense of adventure and trust.

❓ How to Play

Lie down on your back on a soft rug. Hold your baby firmly above you and lift your baby up and down and sideways. Go slowly at first, and watch your baby's face carefully to make sure that she is smiling and not afraid. Some babies do not like to be held aloft, and if this is the case with your baby, then try another game. Your baby will like it if you add airplane noises or other sound effects. Stop when your arms get tired—even though your baby may want to play more.

🕐 Where and When

This is another game you will likely play a lot, anywhere, anytime.

🍎 What You Are Teaching

This game helps your baby gain body strength, plus she'll learn balance—and trust.

🍼 What You Need

You just need strong arms!

Birth + Heads Up Game

Because experts now recommend that babies be put to sleep on their backs, they don't get as much "tummy time" as earlier generations of babies. This game helps ensure your baby gets the opportunity to build his strength by playing on his tummy.

❓ How to Play

Put your baby on his tummy on the floor. For a very young baby, guide him so that he turns his head to the side. As he gets older, he will lift his head to see what's happening around him, and eventually he'll push up with his arms and figure out how to crawl. To encourage the first "heads up," sit with your baby, talk to him, sing with him, and show him toys. Encourage him to lift his head to see and respond to you.

Where and When
Play this game at home when your baby is alert.

What You Are Teaching
This game encourages body awareness and strength building.

What You Need
You can use a blanket on the floor and have some of your baby's toys nearby.

 Balance Ball Game

Many adults use a balance ball to build strength. If you have one, you can use it to help your baby build her strength and sense of balance, too. Or you can use a smaller rubber ball instead. Always do this exercise on a soft rug or mat in the off chance that your baby slips from your grip.

How to Play
Holding your baby gently but securely, sit her on the balance ball. Keep your hands around her waist and back as she wobbles a little on the ball. As she gets stronger and is more able to balance on the ball, hold her hands instead of her body. This is a great game for building her core muscle strength.

Where and When
Play this game at home when your baby is playful and alert. Right after eating may not be the best time.

What You Are Teaching
Your baby gains balance and body awareness.

What You Need
You need a balance or exercise ball.

 Just-So Sitting Game

In this activity, position your baby "just so" and he'll be able to sit unsupported for a little while. Try this after you've done the "Sitting Around Game," explained earlier, and he'll appear ready to start practicing how to sit without the pillows.

How to Play

Sit your baby on the floor. Spread his legs into a "V." Put his hands together and place them palms down on the floor between his legs. To reach the floor, he'll need to lean over a bit. Support him at first, then let go and see if he can maintain the position by himself. Always supervise your baby when he's trying this activity.

If your baby is already sitting unsupported, you can slowly improve his strength and coordination by playing with him in this position. You can play games like "patty-cake," "peek-a-boo," or place a soft toy or ball in front of your baby for him to pick up.

Where and When

This activity can be done anywhere, when you're playing on the floor.

What You Are Teaching

Your baby is learning balance and building strength.

What You Need

You don't need anything special for this activity—a blanket for the floor is optional.

3+ months Baby Sit-Ups Game

This activity gets your baby doing little sit-ups. Because young babies can't hold their heads up, be sure to support your baby's head and neck as you do this activity.

How to Play

Lay your baby on her back. Facing her, slide your hands under her, with one arm supporting her head and neck and the other supporting her back. Gently pull your baby up toward you, then lower her back down. Look at her and talk or sing as you slowly move her up and down.

Where and When
This activity can be played on the floor or bed, anytime.

What You Are Teaching
Your baby gains body awareness and balance and builds muscles.

What You Need
You don't need anything special—a blanket for the floor is optional.

3+ months Gentle Pull-Ups Game

Most babies are around six to eight months old before they can sit unsupported. This game helps your baby gain the necessary muscle strength needed to sit by himself.

How to Play
With your baby on his back, take his hands and gently pull him up into a sitting position. He will lift his head and try to help if he's ready. If he doesn't try to lift his head and help, gently return him to his lying position and try again another time.

Where and When
Play pull-ups on the floor or in bed when your baby is alert and playful.

What You Are Teaching
Your baby gains muscle strength and balance.

What You Need
No special equipment is needed for gentle pull-ups.

Birth + Arm Stretch Game

Stretching games are great because they help young babies move their limbs, which they don't have good control over and can't coordinate movement of on their own yet.

How to Play

With your baby lying on her back, gently stretch her arms over her head and back down again. You can also bring her arms together over her head and back down again. Sing or talk to your baby as you play this game.

Where and When

Play on the floor, bed, or couch anytime your baby is willing.

What You Are Teaching

This game teaches your baby body awareness and builds strength.

What You Need

All you need is a soft surface for your baby to lie on.

3+ months Leg Stretch Game

As your baby gets stronger, he'll probably push back or kick his legs when you play this game. Encourage his movements!

How to Play

With your baby on his back, bend his knee, then gently push his leg toward his torso. Gently stretch it back down. Talk or sing to him while you're doing the stretch.

Where and When

Do leg stretches anywhere, anytime your baby is willing.

What You Are Teaching

Your baby is building strength and body awareness.

What You Need

All you need is a soft spot for your baby to lie on.

3-6+ months Body Stretch Game

This game works all of your baby's limbs as you play. Remember to stretch carefully and gently, and stop if your baby doesn't seem to like it.

How to Play

With your baby on her back, bring one of her arms up and gently stretch it over her head while stretching the opposite leg down. Repeat with her other arm and leg.

Where and When

Stretch your baby anywhere, anytime she is willing.

What You Are Teaching

Your baby learns body awareness and builds strength.

What You Need

No special equipment is needed.

6+ months Roll the Toy Game

This is a fun game for interacting with your baby as he's learning to sit unsupported.

How to Play

Sit with your legs spread in a "V." Sit your baby facing you between your feet so he can grab your legs for support. Put a pillow or bolster behind his back to help him sit up if he needs the extra support. Roll the toy toward your baby. Encourage him to reach for it and roll it back.

Where and When

Roll toys back and forth on the floor during playtime.

What You Are Teaching

This game helps build your baby's balance, motor skills, and strength.

What You Need

You need toys that roll, such as a ball or a truck, and a pillow or bolster pillow, if necessary.

 # Roll the Baby Game

This game helps your baby learn to roll by showing her how to move from her back to her side. Remember to be gentle and to stop the game if she doesn't seem to like it.

How to Play

Put your baby on her back on a blanket. Very carefully lift the blanket so that she slowly rolls onto her side. Or you can use your hands to guide her over onto her side.

Where and When

Play this game on the floor away from any stairs, and play when your baby is willing.

What You Are Teaching

The rolling motion helps your baby build balance, body awareness, and motor skills.

What You Need

You need a blanket or big towel.

The Least You Need to Know

- ◆ Your baby wants to know how to use her body, and you can help her gain control over it.

- ◆ By playing games and doing physical movements with your baby, you encourage him to build his strength.

- ◆ A young baby needs your help to move her arms and legs.

- ◆ Balance is as important to your baby's motor skills as muscle strength.

Teaching Eye-Hand and Arm-Hand Coordination

In This Chapter

- ◆ Encouraging your baby to grasp objects
- ◆ Showing your baby how to master fine motor skills while helping you with household tasks
- ◆ Helping your baby understand how to let go of objects and transfer them from hand to hand
- ◆ Developing eye-hand coordination through simple games and activities
- ◆ Interacting with your baby in ways that encourage the building of motor skills

We take eye-hand and arm-hand coordination for granted as adults, but these are important skills a baby must develop. In this chapter, we provide games and activities to play with your baby to teach him how to make his eyes and hands work together. We also give you games and activities that will help you teach your baby how to bat, pinch, and grasp objects; transfer them from hand to hand; and put an object down to pick up another.

Not only do these skills help your baby learn to manipulate the world around him, but some of them actually help him learn to crawl and walk.

 Scrub the Potato Game

This game not only teaches your baby some useful fine motor skills, it also makes him feel like he's helping you.

How to Play

Standing at the sink with your baby (he may need to stand on a stepstool to reach), give him a small potato to scrub while you scrub one yourself. Sing a song about cleaning vegetables for dinner while you work.

Where and When

Play this game in the kitchen while preparing a meal.

What You Are Teaching

Your baby is developing eye-hand coordination and fine motor skills.

What You Need

You need small potatoes, such as red or fingerling; and a sponge, vegetable brush, or dishcloth.

12+ months Stirring Game

This is another game that encourages your baby to develop fine and gross motor skills while also contributing to the household chores.

How to Play

Give your baby a wooden spoon and encourage her to stir something that needs mixing, like eggs you're using to make scrambled eggs. She's sure to make a mess, so aprons and dishcloths may come in handy. Your baby can also help you pour as well as stir ingredients together.

Where and When

Play in the kitchen when you're preparing for a meal. Be sure it's a meal where you have plenty of time to let your baby help you prepare it.

What You Are Teaching

This game promotes your baby's eye-hand coordination and fine and gross motor skills.

What You Need

You need a large wooden mixing spoon and food to be stirred.

14+ months Decorating Dinner Game

Let your baby show his artistic side with this fun game. Use your imagination, too, to find ways to let him decorate the meal.

How to Play

Let your baby "decorate" dinner by giving him some finishing touches to perform—for example, arranging pickle slices on sandwiches, drawing a smiley face with ketchup on a hamburger bun, dotting the mashed potatoes with peas, and any other idea that strikes your and his fancy. He'll enjoy feeling like he's helping you fix a meal.

Where and When

Play in the kitchen when preparing a meal.

What You Are Teaching

Your baby is learning eye-hand coordination and social skills.

What You Need

Use simple items you already will be serving with the meal.

Separating Food Game

Your baby will enjoy sorting out food into separate piles while she's eating it. But be careful; she may want to sort your food, too.

How to Play

Pick two kinds of food that can be mixed together but separated easily, such as peas and carrots or small chunks of bread and cheese. Put them together on a plate and offer them to your baby. Ask her if she can pick out the peas and eat them or put them in a pile separate from the carrots. She'll have to use her sorting skills to work out which are peas and which are carrots, and she'll also have to use a pincer grasp to manipulate the food.

Where and When

Play this game at home or at a restaurant when you're having a meal with food that can be mixed and separated.

What You Are Teaching

This game promotes eye-hand coordination, fine motor skills, and sorting skills.

What You Need

You need to have two distinctive foods that your baby likes to eat.

12+ Stamping Game

If you're a crafty type, you may already have a supply of stamps and ink pads. If not, you can readily find them at hobby stores. Be sure to start with stamps large enough for your baby to easily grasp. Don't forget to use nontoxic ink!

How to Play

Show your baby an ink stamp and let him explore it. Open the inkpad and guide his hand so that he inks the stamp. Press the stamp on the page and show him the result. He'll soon pick up the process and enjoy the game. Remind him not to put the stamps in his mouth.

Where and When

Play this game at home, anytime.

What You Are Teaching

This game promotes your baby's eye-hand coordination and artistic abilities.

What You Need

You will need paper and stamps with simple designs on them that your baby can recognize, such as letters, numbers, or animals. Use a nontoxic ink stamping pad, preferably in a bold color your baby will like.

9+ months Stacking Game

For this game, start with simple objects that can be put on top of each other. As your baby gets more skilled, you can give her a set of stacking rings to put on a base in order of size, or items that nest together (like measuring spoons), to teach concepts such as "bigger than" and "smaller than."

How to Play

Show your baby some stackable objects and start stacking them up. At first she'll want to knock down your structure. Let her! She'll enjoy interacting with you and exploring what happens when you knock objects over. Use concrete words to describe what's happening: "See the tower fall. The blocks fell down. Should we pick the blocks up?"

Eventually she will want to stack the toys like you're doing, especially if you encourage her with your words. "Look how tall! How many can Tammy stack?"

Where and When

This is fun activity to play anywhere, anytime you have items that will safely stack up.

What You Are Teaching

Your baby learns eye-hand coordination and about spatial relationships.

What You Need
You need blocks or other objects that can be stacked.

 # Dumping Out and Putting Back Game

Your baby will be able to dump things out more easily than he can put things back in, but encourage him to do both. Dumping (or pouring) things out and putting things back in teaches your baby about sizes and shapes, the concepts of empty and full, and spatial relationships—not to mention developing the motor skills needed to dump and to fill.

 How to Play
Give your baby a plastic bowl and fill it with small objects that are light and soft. Show him how to dump them out (he will probably be able to figure this out without your help). Then show him how to fill the bowl back up again. He will likely want to do this over and over again.

 Where and When
Your baby will likely want to play this game anywhere, anytime he gets his hands on a bowl full of something! It's an easy game to play anywhere you have the right components on hand.

 What You Are Teaching
This game teaches your baby eye-hand coordination and fine and gross motor skills.

 What You Need
Use a plastic bowl or box, light enough for your baby to pick up; and small objects such as little toys, blocks, and rattles. Be sure not to use objects that would pose a choking hazard.

6+ months Can You Hold Two Game

Your baby needs to learn how to pass objects from one hand to the other, and this game helps her practice. She'll also learn how to hold two objects at once, which is harder than it seems! This is essential for her to be able to do tasks that require her to use both hands.

How to Play

Sit with your baby and put a toy in one of her hands. Then, offer her a second toy, holding it out to the hand that is already holding a toy. She may drop the toy she is holding. Guide her by showing her how to transfer the toy to her empty hand instead.

Where and When

Play this game anywhere you have the opportunity to hand your baby two objects. Be sure the objects are not heavy or breakable.

What You Are Teaching

Your baby learns eye-hand coordination, hand-to-hand coordination, and fine and gross motor skills.

What You Need

You need two small objects or toys that your baby will want to hold.

6-9 months Can You Hold Three Game

This game teaches your baby how to let go of an object in order to reach another object.

How to Play

Sit with your baby on the floor. Offer your baby two toys or put one in each of his hands. Now, with his hands full, offer him a third toy. He'll have to put one of the toys in his hands down to pick up the third toy. Show him how to do this by gently taking one of the toys out of his hands and putting the third toy in his hand. He'll catch on soon enough and learn how to put a toy down in order to take another one.

Where and When

You can play this game anywhere, anytime.

What You Are Teaching

You are teaching your baby eye-hand coordination, arm-hand coordination, and fine and gross motor skills.

What You Need

You need three small toys or objects.

9+ months Drop the Toy Game

Your baby probably won't need any help learning how to drop things, but with this game, you'll be interacting with your baby instead of just picking up the things she drops. This makes the game more social.

How to Play

Have your baby sit (or stand) and drop toys into a plastic container. You can also use a stainless-steel bowl, which makes a nice sound when your baby drops a toy in it.

Use the words "down" and "up" as you play the game.

Where and When

Play this game at home with your baby.

What You Are Teaching

This game teaches your baby eye-hand coordination and cause-and-effect.

What You Need

Use unbreakable toys or objects, and a suitable container to drop them into.

6+ months Play with Sand Game

Most babies enjoy the feel of sand as they play. You can also use cornmeal if your baby doesn't like the gritty feel of sand.

How to Play

Put some sand, or cornmeal, in a wide container. Give your baby some cups and bowls and let him explore playing with the sand. He'll scoop and pour to his heart's content. He may also try to eat the sand, so remind him not to put it in his mouth.

Where and When

Play this game outside or inside on papers or plastic.

What You Are Teaching

Your baby is learning eye-hand coordination and gross and fine motor skills.

What You Need

You need a sandbox or plastic tub partially filled with sand. Clean sand can be purchased at toy stores. Also have some plastic cups, spoons, bowls, and other objects that can be used to manipulate the sand.

 Puzzle Game

When you first introduce your baby to puzzles, pick simple wooden jigsaw puzzles of objects familiar to your baby, and with no more than four or five pieces. Good infant puzzles come with chunky handles to make pieces easier for your baby to pick up.

How to Play

Sit with your baby and show her a small puzzle already put together. Take the pieces apart and encourage her to put them back together. Although you can let your baby do the puzzle by herself, she'll maintain greater interest if you play with her and give her feedback as she works.

Where and When

Play with puzzles at home during playtime.

What You Are Teaching

Puzzles encourage eye-hand coordination and fine motor skills development.

What You Need

You need simple puzzles appropriate for your baby's age.

 # Throwing Game

Your baby will probably learn to throw without your help, but this game helps him channel his newfound skill in an appropriate way.

 **How to Play**

Bring your baby outside and give him the ball. Stand near a container that you want your baby to throw the ball into. Encourage him to throw the ball. At first it may be easier for him to drop the ball. Over time he will learn to throw. Show him how to throw overhand and underhand. Have him move back, so he has to throw a longer distance to reach the container, as he gets better at throwing accurately.

 Where and When

This game is best played outside during playtime.

What You Are Teaching

Throwing is a classic motion that promotes eye-hand coordination and fine and gross motor skills.

What You Need

You need a small ball your baby can hold; a hula hoop to place on the ground; and an empty plastic wading pool, sandbox, or other large object that your baby can throw the ball into.

 # Tug of War Game

Your baby can play this game from a sitting position. As she gets older and stronger, she can stand and play.

 **How to Play**

Sit facing your baby on the floor. Give your baby one end of a rolled towel or rope. Take the other end and give it a gentle tug. Encourage your baby to tug back instead of letting go.

Where and When

Play this game at home on the floor when your baby can sit up unsupported.

What You Are Teaching

This game builds eye-hand coordination, strength, and balance.

What You Need

Use a rolled-up towel or blanket, or a small rope.

6-9+ months Act Out the Song Game

Your baby loves to hear you sing. In this activity, you'll also "show" what you're singing through hand gestures and encourage your baby to do the same.

How to Play

Sit facing your baby and sing a song he likes. Act out the song by using hand gestures to clap, wave, flap, and the like. Encourage your baby to do what you're doing.

Where and When

This is a fun game to play anywhere, anytime your baby is feeling playful.

What You Are Teaching

Your baby learns eye-hand coordination and listening and social skills.

What You Need

All you need is a song that is familiar to your baby.

The Least You Need to Know

- ◆ Your baby must develop some motor skills before he can develop others—for example, grasping with his whole hand before pinching with his fingers.

- ◆ Your baby likes to help around the house, and she can practice her skills while she does so.

◆ With your encouragement, your baby will learn to manipulate objects with his hands by grasping them and transferring them from hand to hand.

◆ Your baby will be encouraged to practice more skills if you interact with her as she "works."

◆ Though some of your baby's games can make a mess, he's learning invaluable skills as he plays them.

Promoting Leg and Body Strength

In This Chapter

- ◆ Building your baby's muscle strength through play and games
- ◆ Encouraging your baby to crawl, stand, and walk by playing games with her
- ◆ Supporting your baby's efforts by making his environment "cruiser-friendly"
- ◆ Modeling more difficult skills for your independent walker, such as walking backward, hopping, jumping, and pulling a toy behind her

To do any of the following activities, your baby will need to build strength, coordination, and stamina, so be sure you give her plenty of opportunities throughout the day to use her body to explore the world around her. In this chapter, we provide games and activities you can do with your baby to encourage her to crawl, stand, cruise, walk, and run.

We also show you ways that you can model motor skills for your baby so she can learn by imitating you. If you have older children, encourage them to model motor skills for your baby, too—babies often respond even better to child models than to adult models.

6-9+ months Bouncy Horse Game

This age-old game is still a favorite with babies. Enlist older family members to teach you some of the rhymes and songs they sang to you while bouncing you on their legs. Let the giggles begin!

How to Play

Sit on a chair or sofa. Have your baby straddle your foot while you hold his hands. Bounce your foot up and down. Let your baby push off on the floor if he wants—this is a great way to build leg strength. Sing a song as you play the game.

Where and When

Play this game anytime—your baby will love it!

What You Are Teaching

This game helps your baby gain gross motor skills and balance.

What You Need

You just need legs and feet!

6+ months Bicycling Game

This game shows your baby that both sides of her body can do different things at the same time. The ability to perform *reciprocal movement* is crucial for your baby's motor development and ability to do many tasks and activities.

How to Play

With your baby on the floor, gently hold her ankles and move her legs as if she were riding a bicycle. Move gently and slowly and talk or sing to her while you play. She won't be able to do this movement on her own for a while, but you're showing her how and building her strength.

Where and When

Play this game at home on the floor or the bed, or outside on a blanket when you're spending time with your baby.

What You Are Teaching

You are helping your baby build body awareness and strength.

What You Need

You don't need any special equipment—just a blanket if you're outside.

Reciprocal movement is an up-and-down or back-and-forth motion, in which each side is doing the opposite motion—when one side is up, the other is down. Think of all the activities that require this movement: walking, crawling, climbing stairs, and more.

6-9+ months **Race You Game**

This game encourages your baby to crawl with a purpose—and it's a lot of fun, too!

How to Play

Put your baby's toy at the end of a hallway or other open area and cover part of it with a towel so that he'll have to "find" it. Get on the floor with him and encourage him to "race" to the toy by crawling as fast as he can.

Where and When

Play this game at home, where your baby can safely crawl on a clean floor. The best time is when your baby is alert and active.

What You Are Teaching

Your baby learns gross motor skills and game-playing skills.

What You Need

Use a favorite or familiar toy and a blanket or towel that can partially cover it up.

Supported Standing Game

This game encourages your baby as she begins to pull herself to a standing position—the precursor to cruising (walking by holding onto one piece of furniture and then another) and, finally, walking independently.

How to Play

As your baby begins to show an interest in standing up, encourage her to hold onto sturdy pieces of furniture to help support her as she stands. (Be careful of furniture with sharp corners!) Her legs won't be strong enough to hold her up for very long, so you can support her by putting your hands on her hips to help her stay standing. Don't overtire your baby by doing this for long periods of time— 10 or 15 seconds is just fine.

Your baby may cry once she's in a standing position because she can't get down again. Help her get down, but show her how to do it herself, by gently bending her knees and guiding her to the floor.

You can also encourage your baby to cruise by rearranging the furniture in the room so that she can move from one piece to another without interruption.

 ## Where and When

You will likely be helping your baby stand quite often once she reaches this point. The best place to start is at home.

 ## What You Are Teaching

This activity helps your baby develop gross motor skills, balance, and strength.

 ## What You Need

You will want to pad the edges of hard furniture your baby comes in contact with while cruising.

Dr. Larry's Little Known Facts

Most babies learn to stand while holding on to something between 6 and 9 months. They learn to pull themselves up to a standing position a little later (a month or so after they start to stand). Between 9 and 12 months, they usually learn to stand for a few seconds, and a few weeks later, they can stand alone.

 Walk with Baby Game

Your cruising baby is eager to explore the world on his own two feet, but he's not quite ready yet. This game helps him move to the stage of walking independently.

How to Play

Your cruising baby relies on holding on to one piece of furniture or another to make his way across the room. Where there's no furniture, he has to resort to crawling. To help him walk where there's no furniture for him to hold on to, take both his hands and steady him as he goes. Let him take the lead and show you where he wants to walk.

Where and When

You can help your baby walk wherever and whenever he's up and wanting to get around.

What You Are Teaching

You are helping your baby develop gross motor skills and balance.

What You Need

You just need two free hands!

 Pull Along Game

For your independent walker, this game can encourage her to build the skill of doing more than one thing at a time. At first, learning to walk takes all of your baby's concentration, and she can't do anything else. But over time, she'll learn to do other things while walking, such as carrying objects.

How to Play

You can make a pull-along toy by tying a string to any object that rolls, such as a toy truck. Remember to supervise your baby carefully—never let your baby play with a string or ribbon unattended.

Show your baby how to walk and pull the toy along, then offer it to her to try. Encourage her to take the toy for a walk.

Where and When

Pull toys are easy to play with anywhere, anytime.

What You Are Teaching

This game encourages fine and gross motor skills and coordination.

What You Need

You need a pull toy, such as a wooden train or a dog on a string. Or you can make one with a toy on wheels and string or ribbon.

12+ months Kick the Ball Game

Once your baby has learned to walk independently, he can start to develop other skills, such as kicking, hopping, running, and jumping. This game encourages his kicking skills.

How to Play

Show your baby how to kick a ball. Encourage him to kick the ball to you. Kick the ball (gently) back to him. This is a great game to play with your older children—the whole family can join in.

Where and When

Play this game outside, anytime.

What You Are Teaching

This game helps your baby develop gross motor skills, coordination, and game-playing skills.

What You Need

A light ball that's easy for your baby to kick, such as a beach ball, is all you need.

12+ months Turn Around Game

This game encourages your independent walker to explore the different ways she can use her body now that she's mastered putting one foot in front of the other.

How to Play

Walking with your baby in an area that's clear of obstacles, turn around and walk backward. Encourage your baby to turn around and walk backward, too. Warn her if you see an obstacle in her way. ("Sheri, you're about to walk into the wall!") Then turn around and walk normally. Switch back and forth and encourage your baby to do the same.

Where and When

Play this game at home, where rooms and walkways are familiar, or outside in the yard or a park.

What You Are Teaching

This game teaches gross motor skills and coordination.

What You Need

Nothing special is needed for this game other than unobstructed space.

 Baby Push, Parent Pull Game

This game is ideal for the cruising baby because he doesn't have to hold your hands or the furniture in order to practice walking. The pushing part of the game also helps build his muscles.

How to Play

Encourage your baby to push one end of an object as he is walking. You can help by pulling the other end. Remember to talk and smile at your baby, encouraging him, as you play the game.

Where and When

Play this at home or outside anytime.

What You Are Teaching

This game teaches your baby fine and gross motor skills and balance.

What You Need

You need a large object that can easily be pushed, such as a stroller or a basket filled with toys or laundry.

Dr. Larry's Little Known Facts

Research shows that keeping children very active for an hour or so a day can prevent obesity and improve their school performance, emotional development, cognitive functioning, and social skills—among other things. Getting into the habit when your child is still a baby sets the right tone for the rest of your child's life.

12+ months March to the Music Game

This game builds your independent walker's skills and adds the elements of listening and following directions.

How to Play

Turn on some music and say to your baby, "Let's march!" Then show her how to march around the house. You can also show her how to march in place. Turn the music off and stop marching. Tell her, "Stop marching." Then turn the music on again. Eventually she will understand the game and want to be in charge of turning the music on and off.

Where and When

March around at home when you can easily turn music on and off.

What You Are Teaching

This game helps develop your baby's gross motor and listening skills.

What You Need

You need a radio or a CD player and CDs.

9+ months Tunnel Game

Most babies enjoy small spaces, which is why you may sometimes find your baby playing under the table or hiding behind the couch. This game uses his enjoyment of small spaces to help build his motor skills.

How to Play

Set up a tunnel and encourage your baby to crawl through it. Put a toy or other desirable object at one end and encourage him to crawl through the tunnel to get it.

Where and When

Play this game at home when your baby is alert and playful.

What You Are Teaching

This game teaches your baby body awareness, spatial relationships, and visual skills.

What You Need

You can buy a collapsible tunnel (these can be found at toy stores), make a tunnel with a cardboard box with both ends removed, or drape blankets over furniture.

9-12+ months Obstacle Course Game

This game helps your baby learn to identify obstacles in her environment so she can work her way around them safely instead of plowing over them or through them. This game can be played with babies who are crawling as well as those who are walking.

How to Play

Set up some toys or pieces of small furniture in an obstacle course so your baby can't walk in a straight line through the room. Guide her through the obstacle course and encourage her by saying, "Step over the block" or "Go around the stuffed animal." If your baby is learning to walk, you can hold her hands as she makes her way through the obstacle course.

Where and When

Play this game at home during playtime, when your baby is alert and active.

What You Are Teaching

This game encourages gross motor skills, balance, and eye-foot coordination.

What You Need

You need small toys such as blocks and stuffed animals, or furniture like a stool or small chair.

Brainy Baby

Your baby doesn't need to wear shoes unless she's going to be walking outside. Experts believe that letting your child go barefoot as she learns to walk helps her figure out how to do it, because she gets sensory feedback.

6-9+ months Can You Catch Me Game

Crawling babies think being chased is great fun, so though this game gives him a workout, he doesn't even notice because he's laughing too hard!

 How to Play

When your baby is crawling, get down on the floor behind him and slowly follow him, crawling. Say something like, "Mama is chasing you!" or "I'm going to catch you!" Then tickle a toe or give him a hug and say, "I caught you!"

 Where and When

Play this game at home, anytime.

 What You Are Teaching

Your baby develops gross motor skills and game-playing skills.

 What You Need

You don't need anything special; just be ready to have fun.

12+ months Step on an Animal Game

This game can be played indoors with pictures. If you can draw, you can play it outside on the sidewalk, too. If you have other children, this is a fun game for the whole family.

How to Play

Cut out pictures of different animals from magazines or photocopy them from a book onto a standard (8½ × 11) sheet of paper. Or, if you're playing outside and you have some artistic skill, draw the animals with different-colored chalk on the sidewalk. Give your baby different commands, like "Step on the red lion." As she gets more coordinated, have her do a variety of things to get to the different shapes, such as hop, skip, jump, run, walk backward, and walk on tiptoes.

Where and When

Play this game inside or outside when your baby is active.

What You Are Teaching

This game teaches motor skills and object identification.

What You Need

You will need pictures of different animals on letter-size sheets of paper or colored chalk.

Baby Beware

Although most babies are walking by around 12 months, many don't learn until the age of 16 or 17 months—and there's nothing wrong with that. However, if your baby's motor skills (gross or fine) seem significantly delayed, discuss your concerns with your pediatrician. She can rule out physical problems and reassure you or point you in the right direction for further evaluation. Keep in mind that premature babies develop skills later than full-term babies.

 Still as a Statue Game

This version of "Simon Says" encourages your independent walker to build his fine and gross motor skills while also following directions and listening. It may also be the only time in the day when you can get him to hold still for a minute!

How to Play

Encourage your baby to do what you do. Stand on one leg and tell your baby, "Daddy has his hands in the air." Then encourage your baby to do the same. Then say, "Daddy is still as a statue." Go perfectly still and quiet and see if your baby can do the same.

Where and When

This is a fun and easy game to play anywhere, anytime. It's a useful one when you need your baby to do something that will help you, like be still and quiet!

What You Are Teaching

This game teaches your baby fine and gross motor skills, listening skills, and game-playing skills.

What You Need

You don't need anything special for this game.

The Least You Need to Know

- Between the ages of about 6 to 12 months, your baby will go from rolling from back to front to walking.

- You can encourage your baby in her efforts to crawl and walk by playing games with her.

- Many old favorites are still great games to help your baby master the motor skills needed to crawl, walk, and run.

- By modeling physical skills, you help your baby learn how to master them himself.

- You can build your baby's motor *and* cognitive skills by playing games that require your baby to know colors and shapes or follow directions while using her body at the same time.

Glossary

audio localization   The ability to figure out where a sound is coming from.

baby talk   See *parentese*.

colic   Excessive crying with no known cause in a baby. If your baby is young (under five months) and cries for more than three hours in a row, three or more days a week, he is likely to have colic. It will go away, and it isn't harmful to your baby.

core muscles   Abdominal, back, and pelvic muscles—the most important muscles that you need to be able to sit, stand, walk, and run.

developmental delay   When your baby hasn't reached the milestones of skill development within the a specified "normal" or "typical" age range. There are several areas a child can have delays in, including language acquisition, motor skills, self-help skills, and emotional and social skills. Global developmental delay (sometimes called pervasive developmental disorders) is when a child is behind in all areas, instead of just one or two.

expressive language   This refers to what a child communicates through speech or gesture. By age five, your child's expressive and receptive language will be about the same, and she will be able to hold a conversation very similar to an adult's.

grasping reflex This is the innate ability of your baby to wrap his fingers around an object that's placed in his hand.

object permanence The understanding that an object continues to exist even if you don't see it. Your baby is not born with this understanding, but acquires it over time. One of the reasons a young baby is upset when her caregiver leaves is that she is unable to comprehend that her caregiver will come back. For all that she knows, her caregiver has ceased to exist.

parentese Otherwise known as "baby talk," it's the way adults in every culture tend to speak around babies, which helps stimulate a baby's language acquisition. Parentese includes short sentences, prolonged vowel sounds, higher voice pitch, and a greater range of inflection.

pervasive developmental disorders See *developmental delay*.

pincer grasp Using your index finger and your thumb to pick up a small object—"pinching" it between your fingers.

prepositional concepts These show how objects are related to each other and the world around them—for example, "in," "under," and "on."

progressive muscle relaxation A technique used to help you release tension. You start by tightening a muscle group (such as your shoulders), holding the tension for a few seconds, then relaxing.

receptive language This refers to language that a baby or child understands, which in young babies and young children is more than they can say (their expressive language).

reciprocal movement This is an up-and-down or back-and-forth motion, in which each side is doing the opposite motion. When one side is up, the other is down.

separation anxiety Your baby's unwillingness to let you out of his sight (which occurs around seven months of age). It occurs because he's starting to realize that he is a separate person from you. At the same time, he knows you're his primary source of all good things. If you leave, he doesn't know when or if you'll return—so it's in his best interest to try to prevent your leaving. Some babies don't have much anxiety while others have a great deal.

transition times These are periods throughout the day when your baby has to move from one activity to another, such as from playing to napping.

visual discrimination The ability to see even small differences in the size, shape, and color of different objects. Developing this type of comparison and contrast skill is necessary for your baby to understand the world around her.

voice modulation This means controlling or changing the stress, pitch, or loudness of your voice.

Resources

If you'd like more information about the material covered in this book, the following resources are the right places to start.

General Information

For general information on your baby's health and physical development, visit the American Academy of Pediatrics website: www.aap.org.

For general health, growth, and development information, visit the Kids' Health website: www.kidshealth.org.

For general parenting information for babies, visit www.parenthood.com.

For a holistic approach to stimulating your baby's brain and overall development, try this book: *Raise a Smarter Child by Kindergarten* by David Perlmutter and Carol Colman (Morgan Road Books, 2006).

Brain Development

For information on brain development in your baby, try www.brainconnection.com.

Another great source of information on baby brain development is the Talaris Research Institute: www.talaris.org.

For information about your baby's brain, visit www.zerotothree.org.

Typical Development

For information on developmental milestones, visit www.babycenter.com.

The Centers for Disease Control also offers information on developmental milestones: www.cdc.gov/ncbddd/child/infants.htm.

The University of Maryland's website also has information on your baby's typical development: www.umm.edu/ency/article/002348.htm.

Developmental Delays

The Keep Kids Healthy website has information on developmental delays: www.keepkidshealthy.com/WELCOME/conditions/developmentaldelays.html.

The University of Michigan Health System maintains this website with information on developmental delays: www.med.umich.edu/1libr/yourchild/devdel.htm.

First Signs also offers information on developmental delays: www.firstsigns.org.

Children with Special Needs

Many books and resources are available that deal with specific conditions, disorders, diseases, and impairments. Try searching online using the name of your baby's special need.

For general information on children with special needs, the following are useful websites:

About.com has an informational site hosted by a parent with children with special needs: http://specialchildren.about.com.

The Center for Children with Special Needs has an informational website: www.cshcn.org.

For fact sheets on caring for children with special needs, North Carolina State University maintains this website: www.ces.ncsu.edu/depts/fcs/human/pubs/#special.

For a directory of helpful links for various disorders and information relating to children with special needs, try the Internet Resource for Special Children: www.irsc.org.

Premature Babies

Kids' Health offers this "Primer on Preemies": www.kidshealth.org/parent/growth/growing/preemies.html.

Keep Kids Healthy has some basic information on premature babies: www.keepkidshealthy.com/newborn/premature_babies.html.

For forums, information on pre-maturity, resources and books, try www.prematurity.org.

Language Acquisition

For information from Scholastic on how to help your baby learn language: www.scholastic.com/earlylearner/experts/language/0_2_helpbabylearn.htm.

The Talaris Research Institute also offers information on helping your baby develop his language skills: www.talaris.org/spotlight_look.htm.

For information on how babies learn to talk and what to do if you suspect a problem: www.parenthood.com/articles.html?article_id=8173.

Cognitive Skills (Problem Solving, Cause-and-Effect)

For general information on cognitive development and cognitive skills in babies, try this book: *How Babies Think* by Alison Gropnik, Andrew N. Meltzoff, and Patricia Kuhl (Phoenix, 2001).

For information on cognitive skills in babies: www.todaysparent.com/baby/behaviordevelopment/article.jsp?content=20060920_152614_3304&page=1.

Social and Emotional Development (Including Self-Calming)

For general information on your baby's social and emotional development: www.babycenter.com/baby/babydevelopment/index#babysocialBkmk.

For more on your baby's social and emotional development, try these two websites: www.zerotothree.org/site/PageServer?pagename=key_social http://babiestoday.com/resources/articles/littlefeelings.htm.

For information on your baby's sense of self-identity and independence: www.babycenter.com/refcap/baby/babydevelopment/6577.html.

Stimulating the Five Senses

For general information on your baby's senses, read: *Baby Sense* by Megan Faure and Ann Richardson (Citadel, 2006). For general information on your baby's senses, check out the following three websites:

http://baby.families.com/blog/babys-5-senses-and-how-they-develop-over-the-first-year

www.enfamil.com/app/iwp/Content4.do?dm=enf&id=/Consumer_Home/Babys_Development/Prenatal_Development/Developing_Senses

www.kidshealth.org/parent/pregnancy_newborn/senses/sensenewborn.html.

For general information on your baby's sight: www.babycenter.com/refcap/baby/babydevelopment/6508.html.

For general information on your baby's senses of smell and taste: www.babycenter.com/refcap/baby/babydevelopment/1477143.html.

For general information about your baby's hearing: www.babycenter.com/refcap/baby/babydevelopment/6509.html.

For general information about your baby's sense of touch: www.baby.com/view.aspx?pid=196&cid=544.

Gross and Fine Motor Skills

For basic information on your baby's motor skills from *Parents* magazine, visit: www.parents.com/parents/story.jsp?catref=AB40&storyid=/template-data/ab/story/data/1066.xml.

Discovery Health magazine offers this general information on motor skills: http://health.discovery.com/centers/infant-toddler/development/motor.html.

More general information on motor skills: www.babyclassroom.com/article-motor-skills.html.